# The Industrial Revolution

*A Captivating Guide to a Period of Major Industrialization and the Introduction of the Spinning Jenny, the Cotton Gin, Electricity, and Other Inventions*

# Free Bonus from Captivating History (Available for a Limited time)

Hi History Lovers!

Now you have a chance to join our exclusive history list so you can get your first history ebook for free as well as discounts and a potential to get more history books for free! Simply visit the link below to join.

Captivatinghistory.com/ebook

Also, make sure to follow us on Facebook, Twitter and Youtube by searching for Captivating History.

# Contents

FREE BONUS FROM CAPTIVATING HISTORY (AVAILABLE FOR A LIMITED TIME) .................................................................................. 1

INTRODUCTION .................................................................................. 1

CHAPTER 1 - BIRTH OF THE REVOLUTION ................................. 3

CHAPTER 2 - BRITISH MOTORS START ROLLING .................... 13

CHAPTER 3 - COGS OF THE REVOLUTION ................................. 33

CHAPTER 4 - DISSEMINATION OF CHANGE ............................. 49

CHAPTER 5 - SPARKS OF A NEW REVOLUTION ...................... 68

CHAPTER 6 - EFFECTS OF THE TRANSFORMATION .............. 90

EPILOGUE ....................................................................................... 108

CONCLUSION ................................................................................. 111

BIBLIOGRAPHY ............................................................................. 113

# Introduction

For most of human existence, people lived in a somewhat similar fashion. Everything that has been produced, from food and raw materials to clothing and other finished products, has been done either solely by hand or with some help of animal power. This was the same across the eras and throughout the world, no matter how advanced or backward the various civilizations were. Yet our lives today couldn't be more different. Most of our products are made by machines and mechanical power, allowing for greater productivity and a higher quality of life in general. That advance was made possible by what we today call the Industrial Revolution. Its start in the mid-18th century signalized a slow but unwavering transformation from a handmade manufacturing civilization to a machine-powered industrial society.

It is hard to overestimate how important and impactful this event was. The effects of the Industrial Revolution touched and changed pretty much every aspect of our lives. It not only transformed the technology and production of the entire humankind, but it also ushered social changes, both in class and gender, as well as in demographics and economic advances. At the same time, it was powered by and powering scientific and engineering breakthroughs. The Industrial Revolution was also an essential step in transforming the world into a global village, as it brought significant progress in means of transportation and communication. All that affected how wars were fought, how people lived and died, what kind of art they made, and how they spent their everyday lives. Not only was this change qualitative, but it was also quantitative, as unlike earlier historical events, the Industrial Revolution wasn't limited to a single part of the world. Its effects spread across the globe, affecting almost all of humankind to an extent unseen before.

Because of that, it could be argued that the Industrial Revolution is one of the most critical events in human history, worthy of every atom of our attention. Learning about it will undoubtedly allow us to better understand our past and the world we live in today. This guide will attempt to explore all the aspects of the Industrial Revolution, from its development and evolution to its numerous and various effects on humankind. However, it is only an introduction to this fascinating topic, as it is truly a subject that could be studied for a lifetime. Hopefully, by the end of this book, you'll be yearning to read some more about the captivating history of the Industrial Revolution.

# Chapter 1 – Birth of the Revolution

To fully understand a complex event like the Industrial Revolution, it is necessary to take a look at where and how it started, what circumstances led to its development, and how they shaped its evolution. Because of this, the story of the Industrial Revolution's birth can be traced to late medieval times in Western Europe.

Until the late $15^{th}$ and early $16^{th}$ centuries, Europe wasn't much different from the rest of the world. It relied on human and animal power to manufacture everything. It was mostly an agrarian society, where the urban population, even in the most developed nations, rarely constituted over 20 percent of the total populace. At the time, the most developed region of Europe was Italy, followed closely by Spain. At the forefront of manufacturing was northern Italy, which had gone through a hasty development as a pioneer of the Renaissance. The artisanship of the Italian masters was unprecedented in Europe, and their merchants managed to earn hefty profits through their trade with Asian partners. This allowed for an influx of wealth and goods, which was needed to create a fertile ground for innovations. The Renaissance, although it is mostly remembered today for its artistic aspect, brought the rise of two important ideas. One was the seed of capitalism, an economic system based on the private ownership of the means of production. This system was aimed at only generating profits, with a free competitive market, capital accumulation, and wage labor as its central characteristics. Of course, the Italian cities of the Renaissance didn't develop capitalism in its true form. Still, the idea of following profits as being vital for achieving financial gain did originate among the Italian merchants.

The other important aspect of the Renaissance was the liberation of thinking from the clutches of the Church. The Renaissance saw a revival of interests in natural laws, science, and philosophy based on the works of thinkers from the ancient era. This proved to be a crucial moment for European society as a whole, as it allowed for the emergence of the so-called Scientific Revolution by the late 16th century. This was marked by the birth of scientific thought and methods based on empiricism and experiments. However, it was somewhat obstructed by the Church, which saw this movement as an opposition to its religious interpretation of reality. Yet by the 17th century, it was clear that science was gaining momentum, with more and more breakthroughs happening and more of nature being explained through scientific laws. Besides the Scientific Revolution, the 16th century also brought the Age of Discovery, which was led by the Portuguese and the Spaniards. They discovered naval routes across the world's oceans, connecting Europe with Far East Asia, India, Africa, and the newly discovered Americas. The Spaniards and the Portuguese managed to take over the economic leadership from the Italians by finding naval routes that connected directly with the Far Eastern nations, allowing them to form vast colonial empires.

By the mid-16th century, it seemed that these two countries would become the leaders in both wealth and technology, as no one could rival them at sea. However, other nations weren't eager to play a supportive role. Enticed by the lucrative spice trade that put the Spaniards on top of the European countries, others looked for a way to join in. The first to be able to challenge the Spanish thalassocracy was the Dutch. They were already seasoned traders that played a vital role in the North European trade, but by the late 16th century, the Spanish tried to push them out of business. The two nations engaged in war, adding yet another incentive to the Dutch contesting Spanish supremacy, despite the fact that the Spanish grand colonial empire seemed impregnable. However, the Dutch, who were pressured by this conflict yet influenced by the ideas of profit, were the ones to create the earliest form of modern capitalism. This can be seen in the famed Dutch East India Company. Established in the early 17th century, it relished the idea of turning a huge profit through the control of the means of production and free trade. In fact, it became the earliest multinational corporation, a conglomerate that quickly diversified into multiple commercial and industrial activities, including both commerce and the production of goods. On top of that, it pioneered the idea of shareholders and shared capital investments.

*A naval battle between the Spanish and the Dutch fleets.*
*Source: https://commons.wikimedia.org*

With the upsurge in the trade and economy, the Dutch Golden Age had begun. The increased wealth brought the influx of skilled workers, artists, and scientists to the Dutch Republic. In turn, that caused the proliferation of various manufacturing businesses, most notably shipbuilding and sugar refineries. The development of these proto-industries was also eased by the availability of the cheap energy from windmills and faster and better transport connections via canals, which covered a significant portion of the Dutch lands. Another important aspect of the Dutch era of prosperity can also be traced to their Protestant beliefs, which highly regarded hard-working ethics, education, and frugality. Combined with capitalist ideas, the already-existing high level of urbanization, massed skilled labor, the excess of capital, and technological advances, it seems that the Dutch had all the necessary requirements to kickstart an industrial revolution. They even exhibited some signs of achieving this with the invention of the wind-powered sawmill. This allowed for increased shipbuilding production, as well as other wood-crafted products. Despite that, the Dutch were unable to make the last leap toward a fully formed industrial revolution.

The final step toward the fundamental manufacturing transformation was eventually made by the British. They also had some of the prerequisites that were ticked off by the Dutch. By the end of the 17th century, Britain saw an upsurge in the urbanization of the country, though it wasn't on the same level as the Dutch. The British quickly learned and adopted the ideas of capitalism, forming their own British East India Company on the same grounds as the Dutch. That allowed them to break into the world trade, steadily gaining protectorates and colonies around the world. With that came an influx of wealth and commodities, which, in turn, allowed for the rise of skilled labor and scientific developments. Some of the artisans and inventions were, in fact, imported from the Dutch. Moreover, like them, the English were also mostly Protestant, making their society slightly thriftier and more educated with a strong work ethic, at least when compared with the rest of Europe. It's worth noting that geography also played a role. Britain had extensive coastlines, and many of its rivers were navigable, which allowed for efficient water transport like the Dutch canals. The question is, what did Britain have that was different from other nations that allowed them to spark the motor of industry?

*Navy of the British East India Company.*
*Source: https://commons.wikimedia.org*

The first important factor was the so-called British Agricultural Revolution. Since the mid-16th century, British farmers slowly began to increase their output, producing slightly more each year. This advancement was brought by technological changes like crop rotation, the improved plow, expansion of cultivated land, the creation of larger farms, and new types of crops. Of course, these advances were not limited only to England. For example, the Dutch, inspired by the Chinese design, first devised the improved plow. However, it seems that the British feudal lords were more eager to support and even push these changes in their search for an increase in production and profit. They were only further enticed by the growing demand of the newly formed unified British market, which came about after the union of England and Scotland. Thus, most of the agricultural advances were felt in Britain, surpassing the pace of development in the rest of Europe. The effects of this leap forward in production were twofold. Firstly, it meant fewer people were needed to work on a farm while still producing more food than before. Many villagers lost their small farms, which then merged into larger units, while there were fewer jobs for the auxiliary and seasonal workforce. The liberation of the workforce from farming led to migration toward towns, where many villagers sought their fortunes.

However, the excess workforce in urban areas wasn't caused solely by the migrations. Another contributing factor was population growth. Both the increased food production and the Agricultural Revolution, as well as gradual advances in medicine and hygiene, caused a gradual demographic rise. Once again, other European countries also managed to break the population deadlock that had lasted since antiquity. Still, England once again proved to be at the forefront of these changes. Some recent estimates tell us that from 1500 to 1650, Britain's population more than doubled. This trend in the increase of population continued later on, further fueled by the Industrial Revolution. Another contributing factor to the demographic influx was the fact that since the unification of Great Britain in the early 18th century, Britain saw a prolonged era of peace on its own soil, unlike mainland Europe, where wars were more or less a constant occurrence. Of course, this doesn't mean that the British weren't involved in warfare. However, their land was largely spared from destruction, and the population didn't experience the added burden of civilian casualties. In turn, the lack of military operations and war destruction on British soil also meant that its production, trade, and economy sustained less strain and disruption than its European counterparts did.

Another aspect of Britain's development during the 17th century was that it began turning into a nation with a high-wage economy. The income of the laborers across Europe peaked during the 14th century, as the plague caused a sharp drop in the population, leaving a considerable gap in the necessary workforce. However, as the population rebounded, the wages across the continent dropped. English workers suffered the same faith. However, during the 17th century, this changed. Due to the growing urbanization, increase in manufacturing production, and the success of the expanding British commercial dominion, England's wages started to rise again. At first, this was localized to London, then other vital ports, before spreading to the rest of the country. Unlike during the Black Death, the increase in income in the 17th century was caused by the growing demand in labor, making the growth economically healthier and more sustainable. It is important to note that the wages mentioned here aren't measured in currency, as those are prone to inflation and changes in value, making them somewhat arbitrary in such calculations. The basis used here is so-called real wages, which is measured in the amount of food and commodities that could be bought from a worker's salary.

Until the late 16$^{th}$ and early 17$^{th}$ centuries, British workers had a similar buying power as the rest of Europe and even across other relatively developed nations. For example, at the turn of the century, workers in both London and Florence could sustain two persons for a year with their annual income. At the same time, laborers in Vienna, Delhi, and Beijing could feed roughly 1.5 persons, while in the commercially bustling Amsterdam, one's wage was high enough to feed more than 2.5 people. By the turn of the next century, there was a clear shift in the workers' buying power. Londoners could sustain more than three people on a single salary, while the rest of the world saw a drop in real wages. Florence and Delhi were below 1.5, while workers in Vienna and Beijing could barely feed themselves. Amsterdam was also near the quota of about three persons per salary. However, Dutch wages stagnated and even began to show signs of decrease. This disparity only grew when England finally entered into the Industrial Revolution. The reasons why high wages were important are numerous. A higher income meant more food, which led to a healthier and longer life, allowing for the continued growth of the population. Simultaneously, with more money, the workers were able to expand their education and working skills, which only led to further advances in the economy and society in general.

Finally, the last and questionably most crucial effect of the higher wages was the birth of consumerism. With excess income at their disposal, British workers were able to spend more money on non-necessary commodities, like more expensive and nutritious food, better clothing, paintings, and various manufactured goods. In turn, this led to the rising demand for various products, creating the need for more workers to produce the goods. Thus, the spike in consumption began to add more fuel to the economy, opening more jobs for the expanding workforce, which allowed wages to remain high due to the growing need for laborers. In addition, this allowed for the continued growth in the economy and demography. However, it has to be noted that this does not mean that the British workers were wealthy. Compared with modern standards, they were still quite poor. Their diets were mostly monotonous and simple, and clothing and other products they bought were cheap and of low-quality. Yet when compared with other laborers across the world, the British workers were living significantly better overall. In the end, due to the significant impact on the economy, it suffices to say that the high wages in pre-industrial Britain were yet another essential piece of the puzzle that is the Industrial Revolution.

So far, all the listed aspects that constitute this enigma weren't unique only for Britain, even if some of them were more accentuated there. The lingering question remains—why didn't the Industrial Revolution start somewhere else? The answer lies in one crucial factor that the Low Countries lacked—the availability and use of coal. Of course, coal was mined and used for centuries before the Industrial Revolution. However, since wood was both cheaper and cleaner to use, coal consumption remained relatively low. When London began to expand during the 16$^{th}$ century, the price of wood started to rise, as the city's immediate surroundings couldn't supply enough to satisfy demand. Transportation from sources farther away and the lack of availability slowly drove the prices for wood up, enticing some Londoners to switch to coal. However, this was a slow process, as the households needed to be modified and fitted with fireplaces and chimneys, which would drag out the toxic fumes released by burning coal. By the early 17$^{th}$ century, the demand for coal was high enough for its mining to become profitable. Over the next 100 years or so, the need only grew, as coal became two times cheaper than wood.

*Modern-day English canals near Manchester (left) and British coalfields in the 19$^{th}$ century (right).*
*Source: https://commons.wikimedia.org*

The main reason for the relatively low price of coal was that Britain had rich deposits, with a number of them being fairly shallow. Thus, it was available in large enough quantities, and its mining remained somewhat easy and cheap. On top of that, British coal was of high quality, increasing its value. In contrast with that, the Dutch lacked their own sources of coal, meaning they had to import it. The geopolitical situation made it unprofitable for them to switch to coal as a primary source of power when facing the same rising scarcity and cost of wood. Unlike the Brits, they turned to peat as their source of power, which proved to be much less effective than coal. Thus, Britain remained the only nation to depend on coal as its primary source of cheap energy, which, unlike wind or water, didn't rely on the weather for its efficiency. It seems that coal proved to be a crucial fuel for the Industrial Revolution's birth and success. Modern economic historians created simulations and calculations that show that without coal, the British economy would have eventually spiraled into a crisis, and they single coal out as the most essential aspect of the British Industrial Revolution. Even if these calculations and models are wrong, a simple comparison with other economies across the world depicts the same picture.

Nonetheless, it would be wrong to pinpoint the availability and usage of coal as the sole reason why the Industrial Revolution started in 18th-century Britain. For decades, historians have argued about which of the mentioned factors were more critical, as well as over the question of causality and correlation between them. The truth is that Britain was lucky enough to achieve a perfect storm in its economy, as all of the mentioned factors played off each other, pushing the economy along until it erupted into the Industrial Revolution.

# Chapter 2 – British Motors Start Rolling

By the early 18<sup>th</sup> century, Britain was a fertile soil, simply waiting to be sown with the seeds of industry. It had all the requirements for both a qualitative and quantitative leap in the means of production, which would propel the British and world economy into new heights that would have been unimaginable to prior generations. Despite this, industrialization wasn't an easy or quick process.

As coal consumption and demand rose in the late 17<sup>th</sup> century, mining technology started to advance. One of the most significant developments was the introduction of chain pumps, which were powered by waterwheels and used to drain mining shafts. These pumps were not a novel invention, as they have been used across the world since antiquity. However, they allowed mines to go deeper and extract more coal, raising the efficiency of production. Unfortunately, the fact that its primary source of power was a flowing body of water meant that it was unreliable. In the dry seasons, it could slow down or completely stop. It also meant that if a mine was too far away from a river or a suitable creek, the chain pump was unusable. A major breakthrough came around 1712 when Thomas Newcomen designed and built the first fully functional steam engine. Prior to that, other engineers and inventors like Thomas Savery and Denis Papen worked on steam-powered inventions, but most of those were either theoretical or simple small novelty devices. Savery came the closest, as he designed the so-called "Miner's Friend," a pump that drained water using a vacuum created by steam. However, it was somewhat impractical, as the maximum pumping height was rather shallow: thirty feet (nine meters). At the same time, there was also a high risk of boiler explosions. Newcomen circumvented this by using Papen's idea of the moving piston, allowing him to create the first functioning steam engine with moving parts.

Newcomen's design was remarkably simple yet, for that time, incredibly innovative. Water was first heated up in the boiler, then released into a cylinder with a piston. The piston was connected with a fulcrum, the so-called "Great Balanced Beam," which was slightly misbalanced, keeping the piston in the upward position. Thus, the steam wasn't used to push up the piston. Instead, steam was used to create a vacuum in the cylinder by injecting small amounts of water into it, condensing the steam and then leaving an empty space. With the lower air pressure in the chamber, the piston would depress, raising the beam. As the vacuum was relieved, the piston went back up, allowing the process to restart. This type of steam engine was later dubbed the low-pressure or atmospheric engine. The core of this engine was then connected via the beam to a pump, which would utilize the rocking motion of the fulcrum to extract water. It was quite a revolutionary design; however, it was also deeply flawed. It was rather inefficient, requiring huge amounts of coal to work. That made it viable only in the collieries that didn't have any access to running water to power their pumps. Newcomen tried to upgrade it, and over the next couple of years, he managed to implement small innovations, yet he never managed to achieve any significant breakthroughs.

For that reason, most historians don't take his significant innovation of 1712 as the starting date of the Industrial Revolution. It was an important step toward it, but it wasn't widespread enough. However, it diexhibit the trademark mixture of science, technology, and profit that would power the upcoming revolution. Newcomen used scientific breakthroughs in the physics field of atmospheric pressure and weight to generate income for himself. It was a pattern that would be followed throughout the Industrial Revolution. The ironic twist of fate was the fact that Savery was able to broaden his existing patent to encompass Newcomen's steam engine as well, making it rather difficult for Newcomen to earn money from his invention. Nonetheless, by the 1730s, there were around 100 low-pressure steam-powered pumps in the British mines, and their numbers continued to increase. This upsurge was helped by the fact that coal consumption and exploitation continued to grow, while various mechanics and engineers across England continued to fine-tune the engine. By the late 1760s, Newcomen's engine was about one-third more efficient, dropping from about 45 pounds (20 kilograms) of coal per horsepower-hour to about 30 pounds (13 kilograms).

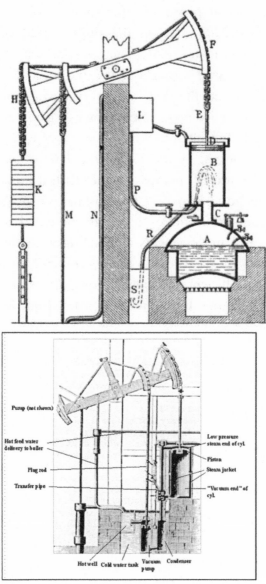

*Newcomen's (top) and Watt's design of the steam engine.*
*Source: https://commons.wikimedia.org*

At that point, two engineers managed to create the next vital step for the advancement of Newcomen's steam engine, and they each displayed different approaches when it came to technological advances. One was John Smeaton, who used the data from a number of working steam engines whose owners hadn't kept them a secret. Through experimentation and analysis of that information, he managed to fine-tune Newcomen's design. Smeaton singlehandedly managed to drop coal consumption from 30 to about 17 pounds (7 kilograms) per horsepower-hour. His work was based on shared knowledge, and in turn, he didn't patent his improvements, choosing to earn his money through a consulting fee.

On the other end of the scale stood the famous James Watt, a Scottish engineer and scientist who, in the mid-1760s, began to work on improving the existing design. Unlike Smeaton, his approach was more scientific, combining theory with experimentation. It allowed him to deduce that Newcomen's model lost a substantial amount of energy when the cylinder cooled off to create a vacuum. Watt's solution for this was to create a separate condensation chamber linked to the cylinder via a valve. This allowed Watt's design to lower the necessary energy by eliminating the need to reheat the cylinder, as it remained hot, while the condensation chamber would stay cold. To further this energy conservation, Watt also incased the cylinder with a steam-filled casing, known as the steam jacket, lowering the temperature loss.

The result of Watt's innovation, which he first patented in 1769, was staggering. By 1776, when he and his business partner actually began building functional steam engines, his machine consumed between eight and nine pounds of coal per horsepower-hour. His design was twice as efficient as Smeaton's. However, unlike Smeaton, who disseminated his knowledge and ideas, Watt impeded further improvements. He rigorously enforced his patent to keep his income as high as possible, banning various engineers from implementing their own ideas to his design. Despite that, and thanks to the widespread usage of steam engines, which were no longer only limited to coal mines due to the rise in their efficiency, many historians tend to use 1769 or 1776 as the starting date of the Industrial Revolution. Steam energy was becoming an ever-important source of power that helped to drive up the production of the British economy. It is worth noting that, by then, other European nations like Belgium, France, Sweden, Austria, and Germany had also built steam engines. Yet the vast majority of them were still located in Britain, effectively limiting the scope of the revolution solely to the British Isles.

Despite the rising efficiency of the steam engine, it still lacked versatility. Due to the fulcrum's irregular rocking motion, neither Watt's nor Newcomen's design could maintain the kind of steady and regular power that was needed for more delicate operations. This meant that it was usable for pumping out water but not for other industries like mills or blast furnaces. In contrast to that, waterwheels were able to create a consistent source of power as long as there was enough flow. One of the solutions for that was to use the steam engine in combination with a waterwheel. In these hybrid systems, the steam engine would pump back the water that had already passed through the waterwheel to a reservoir upstream, allowing the same body of water to power the wheel again. That way, waterwheel reliability was no longer burdened by the dry seasons, and the steam engine wouldn't operate during the wet season, lowering the cost of production. However, this was only a partial solution. Several engineers tackled the issue, yet it was Watt who once again managed to find a solution.

First, he put valves at both sides of the cylinder so that steam could be alternately injected and vented at both ends, creating a double-acting engine. Then he replaced the chains connecting the piston with the beam with a rods system that could both push and pull the fulcrum. Finally, he added the so-called "sun and planet" gears, which would rotate the driveshaft, providing rotary power. To further stabilize and regulate the speed of the engine, Watt also installed a centrifugal governor, which, before that, was used on windmills. It monitored the valves, making the injection of steam more precise. The double-action of Watt's new design managed to produce more power per cylinder size than before, but it also lowered efficiency. It used up to fifteen pounds of coal per horsepower-hour. Nonetheless, the new version of the engine was more than capable of powering various machinery. Thus, in the mid-1780s, Watt's double-acting rotary steam engine began to spread the power of steam into other branches of industry. Interestingly, Watt initially refused to tackle the issue but was persuaded by his business partner and investor that the mills could become an important market for their machines.

The next stage in improving the steam engine came after 1800 when Watt's patents expired. He withdrew his engineers from the businesses he had cooperated with before if they refused to pay for his expertise and knowledge. That left many businesses without skilled guidance. Among them were numerous tin and copper mines in Cornwall. The rise in coal consumption cost them more, as they had to transport it from South Wales. Instead of paying Watt for assistance, mine managers and engineers banded together to improve their engines. Through the sharing of data and the details of their engines, they began upgrading their designs on their own, lowering their consumption from about 10 pounds of coal per horsepower-hour in the 1790s to an average of 3.5 pounds in the 1830s, with some of the best-tuned engines going below 2 pounds. The first step came in 1800 when Cornish inventor and mining engineer Richard Trevithick constructed the first functioning high-pressure steam engine. Unlike in the low-pressure designs, the high-pressure machines used the expanding force of steam to push the piston. This wasn't a novel idea. Watt himself mentioned it in his patents, and up until 1800, he banned anyone from constructing such engines. Outside of Britain, some other engineers dabbled with this technology, but their creations weren't effective or widespread.

*Paintings of James Watt (top) and Richard Trevithick (bottom).*
*Source: https://commons.wikimedia.org*

However, Trevithick's design proved to be effective, and it quickly began to spread. Its main advantage was that, if used conservatively, it could substantially lower coal consumption. Additionally, it provided more power per cylinder size, though running it on the maximum energy output significantly increased coal consumption. That made it possible to downsize the steam engine to be used in other industry branches, most notably transportation. Trevithick himself designed a full-sized steam road locomotive in 1801, one of the earliest examples of steam-powered vehicles. Later on, building upon his ideas and design, other Cornish inventors improved the high-pressure steam engine. One of the most notable advances was the improvement of the control valves, which allowed for more precise control of steam during expansion, maximizing the energy that could be converted to mechanical power.

Finally, Arthur Woolf added the idea of compounding to the design. Essentially, he connected several cylinders that used the same steam. It would first expand in the high-pressure cylinder, then was vented into the subsequent cylinder of medium pressure. There, the steam expanded once again, with less heat and energy, before it was sent to a low-pressure cylinder that used the old system of condensation and vacuum to extract the last bits of power from the steam. By using this design, less heat would be lost, increasing the efficiency and power of the engine. At the same time, the turning momentum became more balanced and uniform, making it more suitable for use in the delicate machinery.

With those final improvements, the steam engine rapidly spread across British industry. This can be seen in the fact that in 1800, water was still the primary stationary source of energy in Great Britain, though steam was used more than wind. By 1830, steam and water had an equal share in power production, while the number of stationary sources in general doubled. From the 1830s onward, steam became the most used power source in Britain, rising to 90 percent of stationary power sources by the 1870s. This explosion of steam power was due to its increased reliability, efficiency, and usability of the newer designs. Additionally, the steam engine was quickly gaining popularity in transportation, most notably in steamboats and steam locomotives. With it, transportation became more reliable and quicker. At first, these technologies were used in short local routes, but they quickly started to expand into transnational traffic, carrying both people and cargo. Another aspect of steam power dissemination was its growing internationalization. With the increasing efficiency, steam engines were no longer profitable only in Britain. Other nations like France, Belgium, Germany, and the United States started to adapt the use of them, though they were still far away from reaching Britain's level of steam usage. Nonetheless, with that, the Industrial Revolution was slowly becoming a global event, one that was not bound solely to Great Britain. However, it is worth noting that it wasn't until the second half of the 19th century that steam really started exploding outside Britain.

There is no denying that steam played a crucial role in the Industrial Revolution. However, it was only one component of it. If steam was the fuel that powered the change, the textile industry was the motor that drove it. However, its beginnings were rather modest. In medieval England, the entire production process was done by hand at home, usually involving the whole family. Like other industry branches, it relied on manufacturing, using mostly wool and flax as raw material. England wasn't much different than other countries, as similar techniques were used worldwide. As for the scope of production, the British textile industry was among the largest producers in Europe. However, it was severely lagging behind Mughal India, more precisely the Bengal region, which constituted about 25 percent of the textile production for the entire world. Unlike Europe, India and the rest of Southeast Asia used cotton and silk as their main textile raw materials, making their products finer and more desirable. Yet, until the European geographic discoveries and rise in global trade, these Asian textile products were rare and were limited only to the ruling classes. However, with the growth of the British East India Company, silk and more affordable cotton started to permeate British society. By the late 17th century, cotton became the most desirable textile material in England, just as it was in the rest of Europe.

Because of that, raw cotton, as well as cotton products, became the most imported items in Britain, making Mughal India the source for the majority of British imports from Asia. By the early 18th century, cotton imports and fashion crazes began to damage domestic producers of wool and linen textiles. They petitioned their government to protect them, as they started losing business and money. The British administration listened, passing two governmental acts in 1700 and 1721 that banned the import and sale of most finished cotton products. These laws helped the traditional textile industry in the short term; however, with the rising average income in British society, there was an ever-increasing demand for cotton. The unintentional result of the said acts was to create a niche cotton industry in Britain, which attempted to satisfy the growing market. Utilizing the fact that the import of raw cotton wasn't impeded by the legislature, a new industry branch was being born. However, since they lacked the skill and specialty of the Indian textile workers, British cotton was coarser and of lesser quality. On the open market, it couldn't compete with the Asian products. Nonetheless, it was still profitable, prompting engineers and businessmen to attempt to improve the production in search of higher profits.

To compete with the Bengali cotton industry, the British needed to economize their labor. As they couldn't employ more people, the only feasible solution was mechanization. The first step toward this was the flying shuttle. Designed and patented by John Kay in 1734, it improved the weaving process, allowing for a single laborer to work the loom. The basic idea was that the shuttle would slide on the weaving board with the help of mechanisms on both sides that would propel it. Before that, because of the throwing and catching of the shuttle, looms required several operators if the woven fabric's width exceeded the average human reach. The flying shuttle partially automatized the weaving process, making it faster and allowing for a broader fabric to be made. However, textile workers, who feared they would lose their jobs to the machines, stalled the implementation of this new invention. Despite that, the increased weaving efficiency only further highlighted the main issue that the textile industry faced. Weaving was already faster and easier than spinning, a process in which fibers were drawn out and twisted together to create yarn. It took about four spinners to supply one weaver with sufficient amounts of yarn if the traditional weaving methods were used. The demand was only increased with the arrival of the flying shuttle.

The first to address this issue was an inventor of Huguenot descent named Lewis Paul. First, he patented a roller spinning machine in 1738. It utilized two sets of rollers that rotated at different speeds, allowing yarn to be spun quicker and more efficiently. He then worked on constructing a hand-powered carding machine, improving the process of cleaning, disentangling, and intermixing fibers to further enhance the efficiency of producing raw materials for weaving. By 1748, Paul patented the first functional carding machine, which used a coat of wire slips placed around a card, a toothed implement used to disentangle the fibers, that was then wrapped around a rotating cylinder. However, Paul's inventions were both slow to be implemented and still not efficient enough. It is also worth noting that all three mentioned designs were also applicable and, in fact, used in other branches of the textile industry. Yet they are more closely associated with the cotton industry, as they were the first step in the full industrialization of its production. By the late 1750s, the cotton demand grew even higher since the British East India Company had problems maintaining a constant supply of it, while, in the meantime, both local and European markets grew.

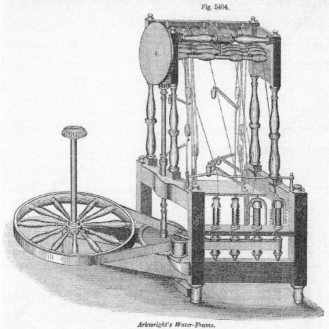

Fig. 5404.

*Arkwright's Water-Frame.*

*Hargreaves' spinning jenny (top) and Arkwright's water frame (bottom). Source: https://commons.wikimedia.org*

The big breakthrough in cotton production finally came in 1764 when James Hargreaves invented the now-famous spinning jenny. According to stories told much later, his inspiration for it came when he saw a toppled spinning wheel that continued to spin on its side. Hargreaves realized that several threads might be spun at once by a single wheel if the spindles were placed upright and side by side. For the next couple of years, Hargreaves continued to improve his design while being constantly harassed and obstructed by angry mobs that destroyed his machines on several occasions, as many of the workers feared the machines would take their jobs. Nonetheless, he began selling the spinning jenny, and in 1770, he finally acquired a patent for it. Despite that, Hargreaves had trouble enforcing his patent, as he had sold a number of machines before it, and many of the textile manufacturers also avoided buying it from him as they deemed his prices to be too high. Nonetheless, the use of the spinning jenny exploded across Britain; by the late 1780s, there were more than 20,000 in use. The machine itself was rather simple and easy to construct, but its main problem was the fact that it could only produce low-quality yarn.

Almost simultaneously with Hargreaves, another inventor and entrepreneur tackled the issue of spinning yarn. His name was Richard Arkwright, and today, he's mainly remembered as the inventor of the water frame, which he patented in 1769. It was basically the improved version of Paul's roller spinning machine, in which Arkwright used three rollers to stretch and thin out the cotton fiber before they were entwined by flyers that spun around the bottom of the frame, simultaneously coiling it onto the spindle. His design was much more sophisticated, but the most critical breakthrough he made was the fact that he chose to power it via the waterwheel. This allowed for the cotton to be spun with much more force while cutting down on the need for human labor. This sped up the spinning process, and it also allowed for the production of much thinner and finer cotton yarns. However, unlike the Hargraves spinning jenny, the water frame could spin only one thread at a time. It was also a much more complicated machine that couldn't be housed in homes. Another significant difference between the two inventions was the fact that Arkwright didn't actually come up with any new ideas but simply combined existing ones that had been used in other industries and perfected it with the help of a clockmaker to fine-tune the design. In contrast to him, Hargreaves used his own inventiveness and constructing capabilities to create his machine.

However, while Hargreaves was unable to further improve textile manufacturing, Arkwright managed to improve Paul's carding machine. Once again, he incorporated the ideas and designs of other inventors, further cutting the time and the cost of spinning yarn. Arkwright's main contribution to this field was the implementation of the so-called "crank and comb" technology, which allowed for longer continuous roving in carding machines. He obtained the patent for his carding machine in 1775, but it was later withdrawn as it was deemed too unoriginal. Despite that, Arkwright had one last major contribution to the textile industry. With his new large water-powered machines, Arkwright realized that previous production arrangements were insufficient. His solution was to move all of the production steps into a single manufacturing unit instead of having them separated by multiple different buildings that could be spread far apart from each other. His first attempt at this came in 1771 when he opened the Cromford Mill. It employed about 200 workers, for whom Arkwright expanded the village the mill was in to house them. For the time, it was a revolutionary idea, a birthplace of a modern factory. Of course, it wasn't the first cotton mill to be opened, nor the first joint place of work for a number of laborers of the same trade, yet it heralded some unique aspects.

First of all, Arkwright machines needed fewer skilled workers, reducing the role of skilled and even unskilled laborers to simple and easily replaceable cogs in the mechanism of production. It also meant that all the workers were full-time employees, who had to work six days a week, usually from dawn until dusk. Furthermore, it sped up the production of goods, as the mill worked on both the carding and spinning of cotton. It proved to be a step in the right direction, for with the rise in efficiency, the increase in income came as well. It also provided safety to Arkwright's business, as there were still angry mobs hell-bent on destroying machines that they saw as a threat to their jobs.

This business model was so successful that by 1776, he and his partners were building a new larger mill at Cromford, while other entrepreneurs and businessmen started copying the idea, creating their own factories. Thus, Arkwright can be seen as the inventor of the factory system, though this title is often disputed among modern scholars. Nonetheless, it was an important step in creating a new social class of workers. Additionally, since both Hargraves and Arkwright created their spinning machines during the 1760s, some scholars use either 1764 or 1769 as the starting year of the Industrial Revolution, as their inventions truly revolutionized the textile industry.

The rising question, like with coal mining and the use of steam, is why was Britain the place where the textile industry went through this revolutionary phase? Why not France, which had a textile industry the same size as Britain before this period, or, even better, India? The answer is, like with steam, the benefit-cost ratio. In both France and India, workers were paid less, making it rather unprofitable for producers to invest in expensive machines that initially weren't as efficient as human labor. In Britain, with the rising wages of the workers, this kind of investment was more than profitable. Of course, other additional circumstances, such as entrepreneurship, the Scientific Revolution, the support of the British government, and the state of global trade also played a role. However, it mostly boiled down to the idea of profit. Nonetheless, Hargreaves's and Arkwright's inventions were merely the beginning of the textile revolution. In the next several decades, other engineers improved on their designs, making their machines more efficient. For example, the spinning jenny rose from the original eight spinning threads to eight and incorporated more spindles as it became a proper factory machine.

*Samuel Crompton (top) and his spinning mule (bottom).*
*Source: https://commons.wikimedia.org*

More important than that was the fact that Samuel Crompton, another British inventor, not only improved on their machines but also combined them into an even superior device. By 1779, he had devised and built the spinning mule, a machine that combined parts of both the water frame and the spinning jenny. Crompton used the rollers to stretch the fiber, though he claimed that he was unaware of Arkwright's water frame, while the spindle carriage moved back and forth to pull the thread. Then it was gathered into spindles, similar to the Hargraves spinning jenny. Combining the two concepts made Crompton's machine even more efficient than its predecessors, but even more importantly, he managed to overcome Arkwright's issue with yarn quality. He added additional rollers while fine-tuning the pull and coiling of the cotton fiber, making it so gentle that a finer and thinner string could be produced. Because of that, the spinning mule was an instant hit in the industry, yet Crompton was unable to obtain the patent due to a lack of funds. Thus, another inventor of the Industrial Revolution saw little return from his ideas. Nonetheless, the effectiveness of cotton spinning quickly rose during the 1780s, causing the increase of raw cotton imports and opening more jobs for weavers.

The next step in the development of the cotton industry came in the mid-1780s when Watt's steam engine became efficient and profitable enough to use in the textile industry instead of waterwheels. The use of steam power in the textile industry was likely facilitated by the fact that both originated in northern England. The steam engine depended on the coal-rich north to be developed, while the cotton industry chose that region for its damp climate, which made cotton easier to work with. It wasn't long before the cotton industry spread across Britain, as it was now no longer dependent on rivers for energy. By the 1790s, Britain was finally able to directly challenge Bengal, both in quantity and quality of its cotton products, slowly taking over the market. However, the British weren't done innovating. Over the years, the publicly available spinning mule was perfected, improving its output by a significant margin. Yet the weaving process remained largely the same since the 1730s. Edmund Cartwright realized it was time to improve it and made the first step in that direction in 1785 when he created and patented the power loom, a mechanized weaving device. His initial design was worthless, but he improved it and patented a new machine in 1789. It was marginally better, yet it still wasn't as efficient as a regular loom.

The main issue was that the power loom had to be stopped to dress the warp, the longitudinal set of yarn stretched across the loom for weaving. Additionally, many of the weavers opposed his work, burning some of the factories that used the machine. Cartwright tried to perfect his design, but he wasn't successful. However, several other inventors managed to address this issue while also making the design more streamlined and efficient, which made the power loom a more viable option by the early 1800s. Despite that, the power loom remained relatively unprofitable and unused until Richard Roberts, a Welsh engineer, patented his so-called Roberts loom in 1822. With a background in delicate and precise machine tools, like milling cutters and planers, he was able to devise a complex cast iron loom. It took some time to develop it further, and the first one was eventually built in 1830. It was reliable and precise, making the power loom more valuable than the hand-operated one for the first time. By this point, the weaving process was almost fully automatized since most processes were self-acting. Yet it had to be manually stopped and recharged when the shuttles were emptied. With this invention, Roberts once again made spinning the bottleneck of the textile industry.

The Welsh engineer was aware of that. Thus, he also worked on creating an automatized mule. Roberts patented the first design of such a machine in 1825 and once again in 1830. Like his loom, it was mostly self-acting, though, in parts of its operation, it needed a semiskilled laborer to work on it. Nonetheless, with Roberts's inventions, the textile industry finally became fully mechanized and steam-powered, sharply increasing its productivity and efficiency while reducing the need for skilled workers. The latter caused great social upheaval, yet the progress was, by then, unstoppable, as in the ensuing decades, other engineers continued to improve on Roberts's design. Another effect of the developments in the cotton industry was that the prices of both yarn and finished products fell, yet the market for them continued to expand. Additionally, other branches of the textile industry began adopting the inventions and machines that were originally used by the cotton manufacturers. It is also worth noting that by the late 18$^{th}$ and early 19$^{th}$ centuries, British technologies of cotton processing began to disseminate across the globe, most notably in the United States. Nonetheless, Britain remained the largest producer and exporter of cotton products throughout the 19$^{th}$ century.

# Chapter 3 – Cogs of the Revolution

When talking about the Industrial Revolution, especially its start in the 18th century, the focus is often solely on the development and use of steam power, as well as on the rise and ingenuity of the cotton industry. One could call them the fuel and the motor of change. However, it's worth paying attention to some other parts of the engine, the less glamorous yet still important cogs that helped it run better.

Among the smaller cogs and bolts of the Industrial Revolution, one can find the iron industry. The technology of metallurgy was revolutionized during the Industrial Revolution, allowing for more extensive use of iron and even making it usable in large-scale construction projects like bridges. Unlike the cotton industry and steam power, which were truly products of the 18th century, the iron industry had somewhat of an early start. According to some scholars, even by the late 16th century, British metallurgy had been organized in a somewhat capitalistic fashion. Laborers worked for an employer who supplied them with raw materials and placed their products on the market. They worked for wages and, unlike the textile workers, had a shared place of work. This was rather close to the factory system devised by Arkwright in the 1770s. The initial transformation of the iron industry came during the 16th century when, due to the rising prices, some of the ironworks began replacing wood with coal, at least partially. However, this caused other problems, as coal introduced impurities in the iron smelted with it. Thus, the use of coal had its inefficiencies and limitations. Initial progress for solving this was made when several English engineers came up with the idea that the coal itself could be processed, similar to when wood turned into charcoal.

By the mid-16th century, after some experimentation, coke became available. This was coal that went through a destructive distillation process by heating it in the absence of air. This process cleansed it from various impurities that were trapped in it. It was initially utilized for heating homes, brewing beer, and other uses that needed odorless coal. By the latter half of the century, the iron industry started tinkering with the idea of using coke for smelting iron. However, despite being better than coal, coke was still not entirely economically viable for ironworks. This changed in 1709 when Abraham Darby I, an English Quaker, managed to make coke smelting practical and profitable. Unlike most other technological innovations of the Industrial Revolution, Darby's development required almost no genius at all. As a young man, he had worked in a malt mill, where he learned about making coke. In later years, he learned that coke was somewhat unsuccessfully used for smelting, giving him both the idea to improve it and the confidence that it could be done. To achieve this, he combined the knowledge and technologies used by others in various fields.

First, he looked upon Dutch metallurgy, which had started to use casting techniques on copper. He tried to mimic that with iron, traveling to Holland and then bringing Dutch experts back to England. Yet it was his English apprentice who finally developed the actual cast iron technology in 1707. Part of that technology was to have iron re-melted for casting instead of using molten pig iron as it flowed from the furnace. Here, Darby once again put in use technology invented and used by others. He used a reverberatory furnace. Once again, this kind of furnace had been used for decades, though mainly in copper and lead smelting. Its main advantage was the fact that the metal being processed was isolated from the fuel itself, making the produced iron even purer. The disadvantage was that it used more fuel to burn, as the melting was done through the indirect heating of the metal. Combining those technologies with his own experience of coke use, Darby managed to create the first functional and viable coke smelting process. However, he was aware that little of it was his own invention, prompting him not to patent coke smelting as his own. Additionally, his initial success was somewhat limited.

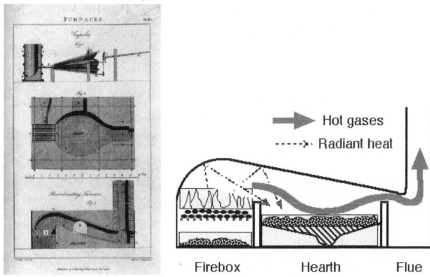

*Reverberatory furnace plan (left) and a diagram explaining how it functions (left). Source: https://commons.wikimedia.org*

Darby's furnace was quite inefficient. His main furnace was basically a charcoal furnace that used coke, which was less reactive than charcoal. So, while a standard charcoal furnace was able to produce about 300 tons of iron per year, his reached up to 150 tons. As if that wasn't enough, his coke pig iron was still too insufficiently pure to be used for making wrought iron. Instead, he used his cast iron technology to make thin-walled and light castings, like pots and pans, which he could sell for less money and earn more. Nonetheless, it was a step that was needed to launch the iron industry into the

Industrial Revolution. After Darby's death in 1717, his successors continued to improve upon his concept. The first substantial improvement began to crystalize when Darby's company expanded to produce cast iron parts for steam engines. This allowed for extra profit, but it also connected the iron industry with steam technology. That proved to be important, as furnace bellows were powered by waterwheels that sometimes slowed down production because of droughts. Thus, in 1742, Darby's furnace used Newcomen's steam engine to power a pump that returned water to the reservoir. With steady power, furnaces were able to work at their maximum capacity, rising the production from about 4.5 to 7.5 tons of iron per week. More importantly, with the higher efficiency of furnaces, the raw ore consumption fell, making coke iron finally price competitive with charcoal iron.

Darby's son, Abraham Darby II, and his partners managed to double the production of coke iron in the mid-1750s when they built new wider furnaces. Their design was significantly better, as the furnaces had more significant volume, but they also cut down on the consumption of coal and iron ore while decreasing the need for labor. From this point on, coke iron was cheaper than its charcoal competitor. Not only that, but it was also more profitable to build new coke furnaces than to convert old charcoal ones. After this point, only coke furnaces were built, signalizing the new era in the iron industry. During the next several decades, various engineers and inventors improved upon the coke smelting technology. Two major advances were made. The first one was the improved air supply to the furnace. During the 1760s, the steam engine was adopted as a blowing machine. In those, steam powered pistons in an air cylinder, pushing the air into the furnace. It made the smelting process more efficient while allowing furnaces to rise in height and produce more heat. The second significant improvement was made to iron purity. Metalworkers realized that sulfur was one of the major causes of imperfections and that it could be removed if limestone was added to the furnace. The addition of limestone would force sulfur into the slag, the leftover product of smelted ore. This improvement was achieved during the 1770s when improved blowing allowed for the higher temperatures needed to achieve this.

These improvements made cast iron even cheaper and of higher quality, finally allowing it to be used as a structural material. The most famous example of this is the Iron Bridge, which was made solely with cast iron. It was erected by Abraham Darby III in 1778. In the ensuing years, the focus was on improving the cast iron refining processes, most notably with the invention of pudding and rolling operations in the 1780s. The former was the technique of stirring the molten pig iron with rods, making less brittle and more purified iron, allowing for low-cost production of malleable high-grade iron. The latter was the use of rollers to create uniform iron bars and beams. It made production more efficient while also helping with the mechanical property of processed iron. Afterward, smaller design improvements were made to the furnaces and blowing engines, but the most critical advancement to the coke smelting process came in 1828 when James Beaumont Neilson patented the hot blast furnace. The Scottish inventor realized that by blowing preheated air into the furnace, its efficiency would rise significantly. It reduced coke consumption by one-third while additionally allowing for the use of raw coal in the smelting process. On top of that, the hot blast furnace achieved higher and higher temperatures as it was subsequently improved. This meant the output was also increased.

*The Iron Bridge today (top) and an 18th-century painting of it
(bottom). Source: https://commons.wikimedia.org*

The end result of this century and a half of metallurgy
improvement was that Darby's furnace smelted around 80 tons of iron
in 1709, while by 1850, an average furnace produced about 4,600 tons
per year. The importance of the iron industry was that its technology
was needed to produce parts for other industrial branches. Most parts
of steam engines were made out of metal from the beginning, while
the cotton industry adopted it as the material of choice for its
machines when metal became radically cheaper in the early years of
the 19th century. Iron was even more important when steam engines
became efficient enough to build trains and railways. In turn, iron
technology was dependent on steam to fully bloom, as without steam
engines, it wouldn't have achieved its efficiency and product purity. As
the Industrial Revolution progressed, metal parts began replacing

wooden ones because of their durability and uniformity. Thus, the iron industry remained an important, although not the leading, sector of the Industrial Revolution. The iron industry also facilitated the development of machine tools, which were needed and used by various professions and industries. Those machines were used to make precision parts, like the one used in firearms and for fasteners like screws and bolts.

Before the advancements of machine tools, metal parts were made manually, using hammers, scrapers, and chisels. These methods were costly and labor-intensive, and precision was achieved only by the best masters of the craft. By using machine tools, these problems were circumvented. Machines reduced the price and increased precision. Among these tools, some of the most notable were the boring machine, the planer machine, the screw-cutting lathe, the milling machine, and the shaping machine, which were all devised and built in the late 18th and early 19th centuries. Thanks to the improvements to production made by these tools, by the early decades of the 1800s, machines completely made out of metal could be built. These machines were capable of mass-producing various interchangeable parts; however, at that time, there was little need for mass-produced metal parts. The only major consumer was the weapons industry, as firearms depended on them. Thus, the effects of machine tools on the Industrial Revolution was somewhat limited. It allowed for the development and advances of various machines, including steam engines and cotton mules, but their full effect was to come in the latter parts of the 19th century with the birth of serialized mass production.

The chemical industry was another branch that was elevated during the Industrial Revolution. Before the revolution, all chemicals were produced in small quantities and had somewhat limited use, mostly in agriculture and manufacturing. However, with the technological advances and accumulation of knowledge, in the mid-18th century, chemical production was scaled up. John Roebuck made the first step in the late 1740s when he devised the lead chamber process for the production of sulfuric acid. He substituted glass chambers for more robust lead in the process of heating saltpeter, allowing the sulfur to oxidize and combine with water, which increased production. That was an important step, as sulfuric acid is one of the most versatile chemicals and is used in fertilizer production, oil refining, mineral processing, and chemical synthesis today. However, its initial use in the Industrial Revolution was for pickling iron and bleaching clothes, replacing the urine and sour milk that had been used for centuries. Another improvement in this field was made by Charles Tennant, a Scottish chemist and entrepreneur, who discovered and patented bleaching powder in 1799. It was made by reacting chlorine with dry slaked lime, which proved to be quite cheap to make and pretty effective to boot. It launched the chemical industry into modernity while also establishing Tennant's business empire, as his production jumped from 52 tons in 1799 to 10,000 tons a mere five years later.

*Charles Tennant (left) and Nicolas Leblanc (right).*
*Source: https://commons.wikimedia.org*

Thanks to the new bleaching process, yet another chokepoint of the textile industry was removed, allowing it to fully bloom in the 19th century. However, other industrial branches relied upon chemicals for their production as well. One of the more notable chemicals used was soda ash or sodium carbonate, which was utilized in the production of soap, paper, glass, and textiles. Since ancient times, it had been produced from burning wood, yet by the end of the 18$^{th}$ century, this was no longer economical due to deforestation. A French inventor named Nicolas Leblanc created and patented a two-step process, now known as the Leblanc process, in 1791 for producing soda ash from sea salt and sulfuric acid. His work was made public during the French Revolution, as the revolutionaries shared his trade secret. This prompted Leblanc to take his own life, but it allowed the British to utilize his technology. In 1816, William Losh built the first soda factory in Britain, and the Leblanc process finally took off. It was one of those rare examples during the Industrial Revolution where the British just implemented inventions of others without making any major contribution or development. Nonetheless, it proved to be an important step, as it facilitated the production of other commodities. The development of the large-scale production of sodium carbonate and sulfuric acid proved to be very important. They enabled the development of various other inventions and chemicals; they also replaced numerous small-scale operations, allowing for more controllable and economical production methods.

Another industry that rose from a humble beginning during the Industrial Revolution in Britain was pottery. Before the 18$^{th}$ century, European pottery was rather basic. It was nothing like the highly coveted Asian porcelain, also known as china, due to China being the largest exporter of the product. Like cotton, Asian porcelain became quite popular, prompting various European artisans to attempt to copy it. However, the secret of Chinese ceramics remained a mystery until the early 18$^{th}$ century, which was when porcelain technology started to spread across the continent. Craftsmen across Europe raced to produce finer porcelain to conquer the new thriving market. In England, the first modest improvements were made in 1671 when John Dwight patented his salt glaze for pottery, making it appear glossy and slightly translucent. However, this was still far behind high-end Chinese porcelain, as the salt glaze was applied to yellowish and brownish pottery, far from the elegant Asian whitewares. By 1708, German potters finally discovered the secret of duplicating this pottery, beating the rest of the continent in the race and leaving the British ceramics industry trailing behind. It wasn't until the 1740s that the British pharmacist William Cookworthy discovered how to produce hard-paste porcelain, also known as true porcelain, at least when compared with earlier European attempts to copy Chinese craftsmanship.

In the subsequent two decades, British artisans quickly developed porcelain technology. They produced refined cream-colored wares, covering its pale body with a lead-based glaze. Creamware, as it became known, became the staple of the British porcelain industry for more than a century. At the same time, the double firing process was also developed, where pottery was glazed and baked, then painted over before being glazed and baked again. It protected the pictures on the wares, and it allowed for the later development of what was known as pearlware, in which the body was slightly greyish and usually adorned with a blue-tinted glaze made from cobalt. Pearlware became increasingly popular in the late 18th century, as it directly mimicked the famous Chinese Ming porcelain. During the 1750s, British artisans developed the technology of transfer printing on earthenware. Using an engraved metal plate, they printed a monochrome design onto paper. Then, while the ink was still wet, it was transferred onto the wares. This replaced the old hand painting, reducing the cost of the product by lowering the amount of labor required to make it. All of this allowed the pottery industry to begin flourishing from the 1750s onward.

This was facilitated by the fact that proper porcelain clay had been discovered in England, while the developments in other industries allowed for British furnaces to achieve the high temperatures needed for the production of fine china. Prior to the Industrial Revolution, such developments seemed almost impossible. However, the explosion of the British ceramics industry is best embodied through the work and achievements of Josiah Wedgwood, a famed potter and entrepreneur. He began his career as a young apprentice, later becoming a partner, of the most renowned British potter, Thomas

Whieldon. With him, Wedgwood learned the basics of the craft, then, using the scientific method, ran thousands of experiments to find the best combination of materials and processes for making porcelain. In his search for perfection, Wedgewood invented a pyrometer, a temperature measuring device used in kilns for increased precision of pottery making. Wedgwood grew and learned the trade, and he opened his own porcelain business in the late 1760s. Wedgewood's workshop functioned in a similar way to the factory system, as labor was efficiently organized and divided, as well as traditional craft manufacturing, where workers had to develop their artisanal skills. In the process, he utilized every possible invention, including transfer painting and the rotating lathe, to speed up and cheapen the production process.

*Josiah Wedgwood (left) and an example of his creamware (right).*
*Source: https://commons.wikimedia.org*

With that, Wedgwood transformed pottery from a small homemade low-profit profession into a fully developed large-scale industry. His experimental scientific side was also combined with his entrepreneurship, as he was the first to establish modern marketing by using traveling salesmen, illustrated catalogs, money-back guarantees, free deliveries, and more. He became so widely renowned that royal families across Europe bought his ceramics. Like his business, which expanded and grew over the years, the British pottery industry also grew, becoming a significant exporter and leading producer in Europe, slowly even overcoming China. Its production became so quick and efficient, thanks to the mechanization of the process, that Asian artisans couldn't compete with its quantity and price. Like with many other industry branches, this effectiveness was plausible and profitable in England since, at the time, it had cheap sources of energy and available raw materials. Even the traditional porcelain producing nations like China couldn't compete with that, as their production methods were first and foremost focused on fuel efficiency.

The construction industry is yet another branch that was modernized during the Industrial Revolution. As previously mentioned, by the last decades of the 18$^{th}$ century, iron became cheap and strong enough for it to be used as a new building material, allowing for new creations never seen before. However, before that happened, another material was reintroduced. Concrete, a composite material composed of fine and coarse aggregate fused together with a liquefied cement, was first discovered by ancient Romans, but that knowledge was lost during the Middle Ages. By the late 17$^{th}$ century, some primitive types had been made across Europe, but the first step toward more widespread use was made by John Smeaton in the 1750s. He created a new variety of concrete using hydraulic lime, with pebbles and powdered brick acting as aggregate. It was essentially the same concrete that the Romans used. It was an important step in construction, as concrete was a rather cheap, easily moldable building material that was sturdier and more durable than wood. As the decades went on, concrete was perfected, and its use became more common. As a result, the race to improve the concrete technology heated up as its popularity grew, with several new types being made in the early 19$^{th}$ century.

One particular type of concrete stood out. It was patented in 1824 by Joseph Aspdin, a British builder. It became known later as Portland cement, as it resembled the very coveted Portland stone. Aspdin's revolutionary process included compacting a mixture of clay and limestone in high temperatures before grinding it into a fine powder. Then the cement powder was mixed with water, sand, and gravel to produce the first known type of modern concrete. It is worth noting that this concrete was different than what we use today, but it was the first step toward it. In later years, Aspdin himself improved upon the original process by adding calcium silicates, making the new concrete more reliable and more durable than before. Others after him continued to perfect it as well. By the mid-19th century, it became the building material of choice. It was even used in the construction of the Thames Tunnel. The next step in construction technology arrived in 1849 when concrete was reinforced with iron bars. However, this invention was made by French gardener Joseph Monier, who wanted to make more durable flower pots. By adding iron bars in the concrete, he achieved higher tensile strength and elasticity. However, it wasn't until the late 19th century that this new composite material began to be widely used in construction.

Papermaking was yet another craft that turned from small-scale handmade production into large-scale industrial manufacturing. The rise in literacy and dissemination of education during the 18th century led to the slow and steady increase for the demand of paper, both for printing and for writing. However, until the 1790s, the process remained largely the same as in previous centuries. Louis-Nicolas Robert, a French soldier and mechanical engineer, made the first step with his continuous papermaking machine. Prior to his invention, paper was made in individual sheets by pouring pulp slurry into a fabric sheet mold. The pulp was then pressed and left to dry. It was a long and tedious process. In Robert's design, the pulp slurry was distributed onto a continuous moving woven mesh belt, through which water would drain via gravity. The belt would then carry the dried pulp through a press, where it was dried and flattened before the paper was rolled into large reels. Robert's machine was capable of producing tons of paper with minimal labor and at a higher speed. However, Robert felt that England was a better environment for the further development of his machine, but as the Napoleonic Wars raged on, he was unable to move there. Instead, he sent his brother-in-law, John Gamble, an Englishman living in Paris, in his place. Gamble found investors, the Fourdrinier brothers, and patented the machine in 1801.

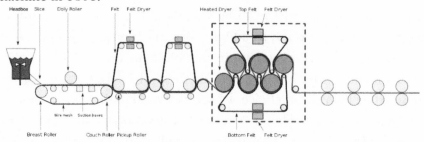

*A basic diagram of a Fourdrinier paper machine.*
*Source: https://commons.wikimedia.org*

The papermaking machine quickly took off, with several minor improvements being made in the ensuing years. By then, it became known as the Fourdrinier machine, meaning Robert lost all control over his invention as well as the profit. Other papermaking machines were soon invented, and unlike other initial designs of the Industrial Revolution, these technologies quickly spread across the globe. This was important because it allowed for the industrial manufacturing of paper, and the paper itself made it easier for education and knowledge to be spread. Thus, publishing businesses were able to grow, helped along by the developments in the printing industry. In that branch, nothing had substantially changed for centuries after Johannes Gutenberg's invention of the printing press. Then, in 1800, the first printing press made out of cast iron was produced. It made the printing process more efficient by reducing the force required by 90 percent while also doubling the dimension of the printed area. However, it was still man-powered and thus was a fairly slow process. This changed when Friedrich Koenig, a German printer, designed the first steam-powered printing press. He moved to London in 1804, and by 1807, he had acquired British partners and investors. By 1811, his invention went into production, revolutionizing the industry. It allowed for faster and cheaper printing. Coupled with industrially made paper, this led to a boom in the newspaper industry, as more and more papers were being printed, and their circulation grew. It was also the first step toward mass media.

Other economy sectors were also improving during the Industrial Revolution. In agriculture, after the invention of the seed drill and the adaptation of the iron plow in the early 18th century, which were a part of the British Agricultural Revolution, everything remained the same for several decades. Then, in the mid-1780s, a Scottish engineer named Andrew Meikle invented the threshing machine. This invention increased the efficiency of agricultural production. Prior to that, hand threshing with a flail measured up to about 25 percent of the labor used in the agrarian sector. It also marked the beginning of the mechanization of farming.

Glass manufacturing was also industrialized with the development of the cylinder method to produce glass sheets. In this method, glass was first blown into a long cylinder, then cut along its length and flattened onto a cast iron frame. From there, soft glass was rolled into a sheet and sent through a kiln on rollers. This method was first adopted by British companies in 1832 and allowed for the production of larger pieces of glass, making it a more viable construction material. That prompted the glass roof craze that emerged in the latter part of the century.

Another upcoming industry of the late Industrial Revolution was the gas lighting industry. As the mining industry expanded, miners began stumbling upon natural gasses as they dug for coal. It wasn't long before they realized it was flammable. However, gas lighting wasn't put into use until the 1790s when William Murdoch began experimenting with it. His initial experiments were successful enough for him to use gas as the lighting in his own house before lighting the main building of Watt's Soho Foundry, where he was employed at the time. By the early 1800s, various other engineers began to experiment on the use and manufacturing of gasses. However, another one of Watt's employee, Samuel Clegg, who was inspired by Murdoch's experiments, made an important step forward. He expanded upon

Murdoch's initial research, improving the large-scale gasification of coal and even the process of gas purification with lime purifiers. At the time, gas lighting was mainly used in factories, but in 1813, the newly founded Gas Light and Coke Company, with Clegg as its chief engineer, was awarded the first public gas lighting contract. They illuminated the famous Westminster Bridge in London. From there on, the public use of gas lighting began to spread. Private use spread as well. With gas lighting, which was cheaper and more efficient than candles and oils, businesses could stay open longer, while the street lights kept the cities lit. As a result, the nightlife scene began to flourish. It's worth noting, though, that similar experiments and advancements were made across the world at roughly the same time, from America to Germany. Thus, this advance, unlike most other ones of the Industrial Revolution, wasn't strictly confined to Britain.

There are many other examples of the advances and inventions that transformed the economy, production, and human lives during this period. In fact, it is just too many to mention. Some of the cogs in the complex mechanism that was the Industrial Revolution were instrumental, while others were less important, but together they propelled the economy and society into modernity, allowing for great changes that led us to the lives we live today.

# Chapter 4 – Dissemination of Change

By the early 19$^{th}$ century, the British economy and society went through an enormous change. Within a century, it had transformed from a more or less medieval form to a modern one, making Britain an economic leader of the world. By 1851, the year of the famous Great Exhibition, a first in a series of World's Fairs that showcased industrial and cultural achievements, Britain had no real rivals. It mined about two-thirds of the world's coal, and it also accounted for about half of the world's iron and textile production. The per capita income of Great Britain was the highest in the world, making it seem as if no one would ever catch up to it.

Despite how it looked to 19$^{th}$-century observers, the truth was that the British economic miracle was slowing down. In the 1830s, its pace was slowly dying down, prompting many scholars to deem that decade as the end of the Industrial Revolution, though some extend it to the 1850s. In contrast to that, beginning in the early decades of the 19$^{th}$ century, other countries began to implement some of the British advances in their economies. This led to a transitional period, which, in a way, can be seen as the second phase of the Industrial Revolution, the time it started to become a truly international phenomenon. Many of the European nations realized how powerful industrialization could be after the Napoleonic Wars, yet the British weren't keen on sharing their know-how with others in an attempt to preserve their superiority. A law from the 1780s, which banned any export of industrial machinery, parts, designs, or any other industrial technology or advances, legally supported this. Yet paradoxically, it was mostly thanks to the British themselves that the industrial seed had spread across the world. Many of their engineers and skilled laborers were willing to share their knowledge and experience for the right amount of money, easing the formation of industries in other countries. A great example of this is the fact that by 1830, no less than 15,000 skilled British technicians were working in the French textile and metallurgical factories.

Besides such expertise sharing, another way foreigners acquired British intelligence was to send their talented students and engineers to Great Britain to learn on their own, after which they would return to their homelands and set up new plants. Additionally, some of the entrepreneurs even bribed and smuggled machines from England in an attempt to duplicate British economic success. Of course, this was only a foothold in the door, as most industrialists from the mainland tried to train and educate their local labor force since they were cheaper and easier to work with. Despite some rocky early years, by the 1840s, there were several new industrial countries, most notably France, Germany, and the United States. However, the first mainland nation to pick up industrialization was Belgium. The roots of its transformation can be traced to the arrival of an English engineer, William Cockerill, to Belgium in the late 1790s. He heard there was a wool industry there. However, Belgium was occupied by revolutionary France, but that didn't stop William from coming. His work was successful, and he even brought his family over in the early 1800s. William's fortune was furthered when he set up a machine-building factory in Liège in 1807. The very same year, Napoleon awarded him with the highest French order, the Legion of Honor. By 1810, he was given citizenship as well.

Around that time, he retired, leaving his business to his sons, with John Cockerill being the more prominent and successful one. John diversified the products they made, which ranged from textile machines, such as spinning jennies, to various steam engines, including traction and ship engines. He also exhibited interests in mines and collieries, as well as textile and paper factories. It was from his humble works that Belgium entered its own industrial revolution in the mid-1820s, becoming an important textile, iron, and coal producer on the continent. Besides the influence of the Cockerill family, the reason why Belgium was the first to industrialize was the fact that Wallonia, the southern part of the country in which Liège is located, was rich with coal that could be mined at shallow depths, just like in Britain. With British mining technology, it was rather profitable to extract it and cheap enough for other industries, most notably the metallurgy and textile industries, to use it. It wasn't long before Belgian products were being sold across the continent. Two industrial centers rose: Ghent as a textile hub, and Liège, which remained linked to the steel industry. Additionally, Belgium, after gaining its independence from the Netherlands in 1830, invested in building a railway network to stimulate the development of the economy. It was a simple system that connected major cities, ports, and mining areas, as well as to neighboring countries. It allowed for the quicker and cheaper transportation of people and goods, which was necessary for rapid industrial growth.

*A Belgian locomotive from the 1830s (left) and a German locomotive from the 1850s. Source: https://commons.wikimedia.org*

Though Belgium was an early contender, Germany turned out to be a much more important economic powerhouse. However, its rise was slowed down by the fact that Germany was divided into several smaller states and kingdoms, with Prussia being the leading one. Additionally, during the Napoleonic Wars, it was under French rule. Despite that, in the decades following the fall of the French Empire, the German states exhibited a great interest in learning from the British, importing their knowledge and skills. However, it wasn't until the 1830s that the German economy started to pick up its pace. First, the German states formed a unified market through the Customs Union, known as the *Zollverein*. Secondly, during the late 1830s and 1840s, Prussia, Saxony, and some other states made advancements in agriculture, introducing new crops like potatoes and increasing their food output, which allowed more laborers to move to towns. Despite that, the German states were still bogged down in traditional production systems, with guilds still having substantial influence over the cities. Additionally, the rest of the society, including the land aristocracy and Church, exhibited disdain for entrepreneurship. That, combined with the complicated state bureaucracy, made it rather tough for the industry to spark. Nonetheless, by the late 1830s, the seed of the textile industry had been sown.

*Map of the German railway network in 1849 (including surrounding states as well). Source: https://commons.wikimedia.org*

During the 1840s, the German states began investing in railways, which additionally sped up the development of their economies. It created new markets for local products and increased the demand for engineers, architects, skilled mechanists, and managers while stimulating the investments in coal and iron production. Luckily, the German lands, mostly the northern regions, were abundant in both. It was during 1840 that the famous Ruhr Valley became a new industrial center, as it was rich with coal mines and home to a booming metallurgical industry. German manufacturing of steel and coal began to expand during the 1850s, picking up enormous speed. For example, iron production grew at a yearly rate of about 14 percent. Moreover, the output of coal in the Ruhr Valley rose from a little less than 2 million tons in 1850 to about 22 million tons in 1880. An important boost to the German economy came in 1871. After the Franco-Prussian War, the German states acquired the industrialized regions of Alsace and Lorraine, which had already developed textile and metallurgy industries. Even more important, the German states finally united under Prussian rule into a single German Empire. Its economy blossomed afterward. All the German lands had the same laws, their bureaucracy was more efficient, and the market was genuinely unified. Most importantly, the Prussian policy of state-backed industry was allowed to spread.

This was important, as Germany, unlike Britain, had a smaller preindustrial middle class and less starting capital. Governmental support was crucial, as it promoted the accumulation of investments that were needed to kickstart industries. Another significant difference from the industrialization processes of other nations was that the German economic revolution began after the railroad network had been established. This meant that there was already a high demand for coal and steel, making heavy industry the primary focus of the government and, in turn, of entrepreneurs. However, heavy industry demanded much higher capital investments, prompting the creations of big companies and economic cartels. A prime example of this was the Krupp conglomerate, which was run by the family of the same name. By the 1870s, this firm dominated the German steel industry, branching from mining and smelting iron to the production of armaments and railway parts. This same business model continued in new branches of industry, like chemicals and electrical equipment, technologies in which Germany became a leader in the late 19th century. Thus, Siemens and Allgemeine Elektricitäts-Gesellschaft (better known as AEG) managed to control over 90 percent of the German electric industry, and they even branched abroad. Those large firms were also combining their interests and protecting their revenue by forming cartels that set production quotas and prices. Of course, this doesn't mean that there weren't any small or middle firms, nor that other countries, like Britain or France, didn't form their own big businesses.

Another important aspect of the German industrialization was that, in the early stages of the Industrial Revolution, their inventors and scientists contributed almost nothing to the development of the technology. In fact, the German industry was dependent on the import of foreign technology and expertise. The German states even lacked a sufficient number of skilled workers. In the 1830s, one manufacturer complained that he couldn't find a single German laborer who could make a machine screw. This lack of technical and mechanical know-how also contributed to the late start of the German Industrial Revolution. However, the German states did have rather advanced and widespread education, as well as their well-known diligent work ethics. Due to these factors, the Germans quickly learned and adopted new technologies and skills, forming a new class of experts for many fields. Thanks to that, by the 1870s, the role of German scientists and engineers changed as they started to develop new technologies, most notably in the chemical industry. Thus, by the late 19th century, the German economy became one of the leading in the world in all aspects, from production output to technological advances, second probably only to the still superior British industry.

A stark contrast to the German example was their western neighbor of France. Since the late 17th century, its inventors and engineers began experimenting with many of the same technologies as their British colleagues. They had similar or even the same ideas as the ones across the Channel, and some of their breakthroughs and ideas were actually copied by the British industrial pioneers. However, France's outdated social system was still based on the same foundations of medieval feudalism, and even more, the lack of natural resources, mainly coal, prevented France from joining Britain as one of the leaders of the revolution. Its position worsened in the latter half of the 18th century when its economy started to decline. What little protoindustrial manufacturing was set up in the various workshops and factories plummeted with the beginning of the French Revolution in 1789. Over the next quarter of the century, France went through tremendous turmoil and numerous wars, which depleted its manpower and economy, preventing any significant improvements in the industrial sector. Thus, after 1815, France remained mostly an agricultural economy with an underdeveloped handicraft industry. Despite that, Napoleon's rule at least broke the traditional economic systems, including serfdom and guilds. Additionally, Napoleon realized the importance of engineering, fostering the development of that field, while at the same time creating a strong banking sector under the Bank of France.

France saw little benefit from those innovations under his rule. Still, it allowed for the development of its industry from the 1820s onward. However, its industrial transformation was significantly slower than any of the aforementioned countries. France suffered throughout the 19th century from numerous social upheavals and revolutions. Its population also grew much slower than those of Britain or Germany. This meant the laborers had a choice to stay in the countryside and work there, making it harder to recruit factory workers. Still, there was some economic growth, with an increase in both iron and coal production, while textiles remained the primary industry branch until the latter half of the 19th century. Additionally, unlike the Germans, the French also made significant contributions to the development of textile technologies. The most notable of all was the invention of the

Jacquard loom, made by Joseph Marie Jacquard in 1804. He simplified the process of manufacturing textiles with intricate patterns, using punched cards laced together into a continuous sequence. The holes in the cards dictated which needles and hooks were to weave into the cloth, creating a possibility to manufacture intricate designs through mass production. This invention brought new capabilities to the textile industry. The Jacquard loom also served as the inspiration for the idea behind computers, programming, and data science. The holes in the punch cards are basically physical representations of zero and one, a principle all computers work on today.

The rocky start of the industrial transformation in France was sped up with the development of the national railway system in the 1840s. Like in Germany, the French government sponsored the development of the railway while simultaneously boosting local growth through construction and other projects. However, the French state wasn't as involved in economic development as the German states were. Thus, in this aspect, France laid somewhere between the British and the German examples. In the 1850s, though, France finally started developing a more substantial heavy industry while also increasing its iron and coal output. Additionally, it became the second-largest cotton manufacturer in Europe after Great Britain. However, industrialization has its limitations, which French manufacturers tried to circumvent by not investing in expensive machinery and fuel. For example, many of the furniture makers standardized a simplified design and production, making it easier to train new workers and increase their output. Thus, they entered into an unmechanized mass production that was somewhat competitive to the British import. However, the pendulum of the French economy swung back after its loss of Alsace and Lorraine, once again entering a period of slow growth and stagnation.

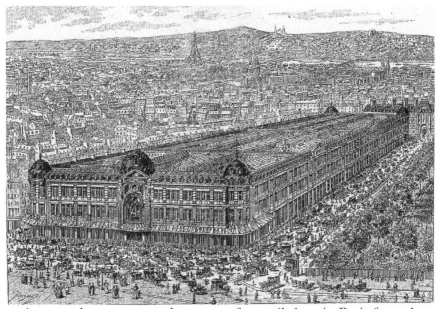

*A somewhat exaggerated gravure of a retail shop in Paris from the later 19ᵗʰ century. Source: https://commons.wikimedia.org*

Despite the slow and dragging development of the French industry, it managed to pioneer a substantial innovation when it came to the economy. Thanks to the creation of the better-connected distribution system, the rise in production, and the growth of the urban markets, consumerism sparked the idea of high-volume retail, which was manifested in the form of department stores. The first one was opened in Paris in the 1780s, allowing the upper classes, as well as the rising middle class, to acquire a variety of high-end products made across France. However, the true modernization of such a model came only after the Napoleonic Wars, which was when department stores began to flourish. There was no more haggling, and the stores started giving guarantees and began investing in advertisements. With the income influx, the stores grew, covering multiple stories over several thousand square meters and employing hundreds of people. By 1860, a single store could achieve sales measured in millions of francs. After a while, some of these stores chose to turn to cheaper products, aiming to broaden their customer base and increase their revenue. With that, the idea of consumerism expanded toward the lower classes as well. Other nations followed their example, and department stores and shopping arcades began popping up in large cities throughout Europe. Thus, it was the French that created modern consumerism as a social standard and an economic force, paving the way for 20th-century shopping malls and the marketing sector.

Across the pond, the newly founded United States was also quick to join in on industrialization. Due to their cultural and historical ties with the British, a small number of their entrepreneurs began importing technologies and machines from Great Britain in the late 18th century, creating seeds of the textile industry as the fervor of the American Revolution began to die out. These new mills were initially powered by fast-moving rivers, so the first industrial centers sprang up in the New England region, which was rich with waterways. In the following decades, steam engines also started appearing, both in factories and in transportation. Yet the US remained predominantly an agrarian country until the 1820s. At that point, local railways began construction, with a more extensive network starting to emerge in the 1830s and 1840s. With the arrival and expansion of the railways, the United States began more rapid industrialization, as it stimulated heavy industry and facilitated trade. Roughly at the same time, a number of canals were dug up, adding another layer of transportation possibilities in the US. By the 1840s, numerous other industry branches were formed, including machines and shipbuilding. Nonetheless, the textile industry remained the primary force behind change, especially as in the late 1840s and early 1850s, a new revolution of the sewing machine allowed it to be used for broader use.

The sewing machine, which is often linked to the famous American entrepreneur Isaac Singer, was only partially an American advance. It had been under development for decades in Europe. In fact, it was perfected on both sides of the Atlantic Ocean almost simultaneously. In that aspect, American industrialization, much like in Germany, was mostly dependent on the import of European technological advances throughout most of the 19ᵗʰ century. Some of their inventors did make smaller improvements on existing technologies, yet nothing really groundbreaking. The only major development in the industrial process came in the form of perfecting the mass production of interchangeable parts. As previously mentioned, the seeds of these ideas were sown in Britain, but it was the American engineers and the US government that really embraced this system. It was initially adopted and developed by the US Department of War in the early years of the 19ᵗʰ century. The department saw its value for the quicker and cheaper assembly of arms, with Eli Whitney, an American inventor, leading the development of such production methods. Within decades, the improvements in milling machines and lathes made it increasingly easier and more profitable to manufacture interchangeable metal parts. These developments led to a so-called American system of production, where semi-skilled workers used machine tools to make standardized interchangeable parts, which could be assembled into a finished product with minimal time and skill.

*Painting of Eli Whitney (left) and a modern example of an early cotton gin (right), possibly his invention.*
*Source: https://commons.wikimedia.org*

The only other significant technological advance made by American inventors was the creation of the cotton gin in the 1790s. It was a rotating drum, with hooks and brushes, which pulled cotton fibers through a mesh, removing its seeds. Its creation is sometimes attributed to Eli Whitney, though this remains debatable, as several American inventors worked on it at the same time. Thanks to this invention, cotton production exploded in the American South, and the US became a vital world exporter of cotton, feeding parts of the European textile industry. Despite that, initial industrialization in the United States remained dependent on foreign capital since not many Americans had enough money to start their own ventures. Thus, through much of the 19$^{th}$ century, industrialization in the US relied upon European investments, most notably from Great Britain. Nonetheless, when the cog of industry started rolling, the American economy boomed. This was facilitated by the fact that the northeastern United States was rich in coal and iron, making the transition to heavy industry much easier. Additionally, until the mid-19$^{th}$ century, the United States was relatively underpopulated, sparking increased interest in labor-saving technology among American entrepreneurs. However, with an influx of European immigrants, most notably the Irish after the potato famine of the 1840s, the lack of workers was diminished, lowering the laborers' salaries.

Regardless of the worker conditions, the US industries and economy continued its development. The only moment when it seemed like the industrial expansion might come under threat was during the US Civil War during the 1860s. However, it only furthered its advance, as the war economy caused a boom in the arms industry, which became an important exporter in the years after the war. Somewhat simultaneously, the US companies turned toward the big business model, similar to Germany, as banks invested in the growth of businesses. As a result, companies, as well as factories, grew, and by the 1870s, some of them were wealthy enough to begin their expansion outside of the US. As big business grew, both the American public and politicians remained in favor of free enterprise, while the government actively contributed to the expansion of industry and large companies. Because of this, many companies managed to form monopolies in specific markets, more so than in any other industrial nation. Alongside industry, agriculture was also expanding by conquering new lands in the West and through the introduction of mechanization. At first, it was in the form of horse-drawn harvesting machinery. Later, steam-powered tractors came into use. With the growth of the agricultural output, the US gained another export commodity. Thus, the United States avoided the British scenario in which industrial exports were traded for food.

Besides the already mentioned industrial giants, other West European countries began their industrialization by the mid-19th century. The more notable areas were Northern Italy, Sweden, and the Netherlands, while Austro-Hungary (formerly the Habsburg Monarchy), Spain, and Southern Italy largely lagged behind. Ireland was only marginally industrialized, as it was under a rather harsh British occupation. Similarly, the US South remained mostly agricultural after the Civil War, feeding the northern textile factories with raw cotton. The speed, level, and success of industrialization in these European countries varied, but they were certainly far behind the leading powers such as Britain, the US, and Germany. However, some overall characteristics spanned borders. In most nations, besides Britain, big businesses formed as the core power behind industry. Additionally, most countries tried to protect their economies and markets with import tariffs on various products.

As the century was nearing its end, heavy industry and the chemical industry replaced the textile branch as the leading force of the economy. Railways connected vast areas, and train transport became transnational. As a result of these factors, the market became increasingly global. The developing industries spurred the thirst for new markets to sustain their future growth, prompting the rise of imperialism. The major economic powers sought to monopolize potential markets in Asia, Africa, and South America while, at the same time, securing new sources of raw materials. This led to a broader spreading of industrialization while also asserting Western dominance across the world.

Outside of the Western world, other nations tried, albeit only to a certain degree, to emulate the advances in technology and production. One of the late examples was Imperial Russia. Until the early 19th century, it was on par with most European economies. However, due to its backward feudal system, it quickly lagged behind them when they began to industrialize. For the first half of the century, the Russian aristocracy was content to retain its traditional agricultural income from large estates cultivated by serfs. There were some signs of industrialization efforts at the time, as some Russian entrepreneurs, as well as foreign investors, began importing various machines and setting up some factories. However, their number was comparatively small for such a vast country. It wasn't until the Russian army suffered a major defeat against Britain and France in their own backyard during the Crimean War of the 1850s that the government began to realize how much it had fallen behind. Afterward, and despite significant civil unrest, modernization started. Most importantly, serfdom was abolished in the 1860s, allowing workers to freely migrate to the cities, while foreign experts and skilled laborers were imported, most notably from Germany, to set up more factories.

*A 19th-century painting depicting Russian peasants reading the abolition proclamation of 1861.*
*Source: https://commons.wikimedia.org*

Despite that, the Russian transition to a modern economic system was slow and difficult. Traditionalism was strong, and the aristocracy openly opposed industrialization. Furthermore, Russia began exporting raw materials, like timber and food, to Western Europe, which didn't require any innovation, causing many to retain the traditional means of production. An additional problem was the lack of infrastructure. Railways were first laid in the 1830s, but even by the 1870s, they covered only small patches of the tsardom. However, by the 1870s, some improvements were made, as the Russians produced more machines than they imported. Yet the gap between the Russian Empire and the West was increasing. The sheer speed of industrialization in the West was just too much for Russia to catch up. But although Russia failed to create a more substantial industry, it was still capable of exporting some of its products to non-European markets, such as Central Asia, Iran, and China.

The Chinese economy suffered even worse. Imperial China, once one of the biggest manufacturers and wealthiest countries, plummeted during the 19th century. Due to its traditional repulsiveness to foreign influence and culture, China refused to adopt any new technologies from the West, retaining its traditional manufacturing system. One of the reasons why it was capable of doing so was the fact that European goods weren't able to significantly threaten local producers. However, due to internal instability, the slowly failing state bureaucracy, and increasing external pressure, the Chinese economy started to fail. In fact, it was due to external pressure that the first industrial steps were taken, steps that included railroads and textile factories, which were first built in the late 19th century.

Thanks to its sheer size and long history and tradition, China managed to survive, mainly ignoring the idea of industrialization. However, other independent nations across the world didn't have much choice. They either had to attempt to modernize their production or fall so far behind that it would be hard to retain their independence. Thus, during the 19th century, many nations like the young states of South America, such as Brazil or Chile, and old

Middle Eastern powers, such as Persia and the Ottoman Empire, tried to industrialize. The pace and starting period varied from country to country, sometimes going back as early as the 1830s. Yet their success was usually limited, with some small local pockets of industry, while most of the lands remained mostly restrained in traditional economies. As such, the majority of these countries remained primarily dependent on foreign imports of mechanical and technical goods and mainly exported food and raw materials.

The only non-Western nation that was entirely successful in its industrialization was Japan. It had probably one of the worst starting-off points, as the country had been almost completely cut off from foreign influence since the early 17$^{th}$ century. Thus, for more than 200 years, it was locked in its traditional politics, culture, economy, and means of production. By 1853, when the US forcibly opened its borders, Japan lagged about two centuries behind the Western world in terms of technology and the economy. To most contemporaries, it probably seemed like the country of the rising sun would never catch up. In 1868, after some internal turmoil, the newly crowned Emperor Meiji restored imperial power, which had been usurped by the shogun. After taking back the control over his country, Emperor Meiji and his government sought to modernize it. Their interaction with the United States, and later with other Western powers, made them realize they needed to bring their nation into the 19$^{th}$ century if they were to survive. To achieve that, the government planned to learn from its competitors. Over the years, they sent thousands of young students abroad to study in various fields, and no less than 3,000 foreign experts were brought into the country and employed on a number of projects. Japanese experts also began traveling around the world, searching for the best examples in every field, be it political or technological.

With this surge of outside experience and knowledge, Japan began reforming. The entire society was changing, with the old samurai feudal aristocracy getting out of the way for the new business elites. A new modern education was formed, and the political and military systems were reshaped, based mostly on the US and German models. With that came the wave of industrialization. The government began building railways, invested in mechanizing mining operations, and gave grants and subventions for the textile and heavy industries. Within years, Japanese industrialization began rolling out. Throughout the 1870s, miles of railways and roads were constructed, while numerous factories and mines were built. Big businesses formed almost immediately alongside them. Many of the Japanese entrepreneurs and businessmen saw it as a way not only to earn more money but also to compete with foreign firms. By 1880, the Japanese economy had begun outputting enough products to compete with the international pressure in its own market, and by 1890, it even managed to compete with Western companies in the local Southeast Asian market. The most notable success of this period was the Japanese textile industry, especially with its silk products. Thus, within roughly twenty years, Japan had managed to transform itself from a medieval feudal land into a modern industrial society, surprising many along the way. Looking back on this solitary example, it becomes evident that the best way to industrialize was with full focus and governmental backing. Other nations relied on half measures and personal initiatives, while Japan left nothing to chance. The results definitely speak for themselves.

*A Japanese painting from the 1870s depicting railways at the seaside.*
*Source: https://commons.wikimedia.org*

However, with this industrial development, the Japanese also acquired the European taste for imperialism. They sought to expand their domain into Korea and China. By then, the European powers, most notably France and Britain, had taken hold over most of Africa, Indochina, and the entire Indian subcontinent. Even Germany, which couldn't colonize before its unification, managed to snag some of the territories in Africa. Alongside these great powers, smaller ones, such as Belgium, the Netherlands, and Italy, also had colonies across the globe. Under their rule, the lands were left void of any real benefits of industrial advancements. The colonizers only brought as much technology as they needed for themselves. For example, they built railway lines from mines or cotton fields to the harbors and also constructed small factories for their own needs. Most of these lands were purely exploited for the profit of their industrial masters. The only exception was India, where some traces of self-made industry appeared in the early 19th century. Yet this was insignificant enough in the larger picture, especially after the 1850s when Britain tightened its reins over the Indian state, pushing farther inland. The result in India, like in many other colonies, was the breakdown of the traditional means of production, with many people going out of business and becoming poor.

The European elites tried to mask their cruel rule and outright oppression of the native population with the maxim of bringing civilization to the backwater lands. However, this was far from the truth. All the improvements they made were for their own gain and use, while the local population was used as a source of cheap labor and their lands as a source of raw material. Industry and its technologies were left out of the reach of the indigenous peoples, though some advances in agriculture did spread. Nonetheless, those advances were usually pioneered by the colonizers to maximize their own production and profits. Medicine and education were only minutely improved, if at all, and their scope varied from region to region.

Colonization ended up bringing more fuel to the European industry, powering the nations' economies forward. Thus, unsurprisingly, by the late 19$^{th}$ century, the US and Japan acquired their own colonies. By the 1890s, the US had conquered Puerto Rico, the Philippines, and Hawaii, while Japan took control of Taiwan and Korea. Similarly, Russia expanded its lands across Central and Eastern Asia. Portugal and Spain, though the latter lost a chunk of their territories to the US, also had some colonies left from their previous vast empires. However, those countries never managed to industrialize, leaving their colonies without modernization as well.

By the late 19$^{th}$ century, the entire world was acquainted with the idea of industrialization, regardless of the will and capability to fulfill it. This kind of change was no longer confined to Britain. Yet despite the advances made by other nations, Great Britain remained the most developed, richest, and most powerful country and economy of the world.

# Chapter 5 – Sparks of a New Revolution

As the Industrial Revolution expanded throughout the mid-19<sup>th</sup> century, the pace of technological advances slowed down, causing many scholars to argue the Industrial Revolution was over around 1850 at the very latest. To a certain degree, and from a singular viewpoint of a British Industrial Revolution, this is a valid point. However, the fact is that various technologies continued to advance while new ones were also invented. Additionally, throughout the 19<sup>th</sup> century, raw production numbers grew as well.

Many still hold that the Industrial Revolution ended by the 1830s because the new inventions that came afterward failed to revolutionize the production output and income. Nevertheless, economies continued to grow and expand. This growth was, however, somewhat impeded by the Long Depression of the 1870s, which was when the world entered its first truly international economic crisis. It was caused by a combination of money devaluation due to the overmining of silver and a stock bubble that was created by overly optimistic investments in new industries. When panic hit worldwide stock markets, people began pulling out their capital, causing stock exchanges to crash and temporarily close. It wasn't long before a recession spread across the global world economy, though it hit Britain and the US the hardest. At the time, it must have seemed like the further growth and development of technologies, industry, and the overall economy would end. Bankruptcies and unemployment became an everyday occurrence in the industrialized world. Yet by the 1870s, a new explosion of technological advancements was ready to burst forth, and new industry branches were ready to sprout utilizing the very same innovations that had occurred in the four decades prior to it. Through these advances, the economy recovered and soared into new heights, leaving a somewhat inaccurate idea that industrialization is capable of overcoming all troubles in the economy.

Before we delve into the details of those new developments in the economy and manufacturing sector, it should be noted that, for many scholars, these advances are seen as part of the Second Industrial Revolution. Depending on the viewpoint, the beginning of this revolution is dated to 1870 or sometimes even as early as the 1850s, while its end date is usually either 1914 or around 1950. Other viewpoints see it as yet another wave of the initial revolution that began in the 18th century. From their perspective, the technological advances, no matter how revolutionary and new, were a clear continuation of the original wave of industrialization. For the intents and purposes of this book, we'll classify it as a third phase of the Industrial Revolution, one that came after the initial birth of industrial technology and its spreading across the globe. In fact, one of the reasons many tend to separate it from the initial industrial transformation, besides the focus on new industries and technologies, was the fact it was polycentric. The advance was no longer contained only in Britain but covered all the industrial nations of the late 19th century, with all of them contributing to the upcoming changes.

One of the most significant advances that revitalized the Industrial Revolution came in metallurgy, signifying that the textile industry wasn't the leading branch anymore. During the 1850s, British inventor Sir Henry Bessemer developed a process that would allow for the mass production of steel to be done more cheaply. He realized that impurities could be removed from the steel by oxidation, blowing the air through the molten iron. Besides purification, air also raised the temperature of the iron, keeping it molten. Known as the Bessemer process, its improvement was the first step toward cheap steel. However, it wasn't until late 1860 and the early 1870s that his process became widely used, allowing it to make a proper impact on the industry. Despite being a British invention, the Bessemer process took off after the famous American entrepreneur and industrialist Andrew Carnegie employed it in his own business in the US in 1872. The sheer impact of this new technology is evident from the fact that Carnegie was able to lower the cost of steel railroad rails by 50 percent between 1873 and 1875. However, it was just the first step in refining the steel production process since phosphorus and sulfur still remained, despite clearing the excess carbon and silicon. In other words, Bessemer's steel still wasn't pure enough.

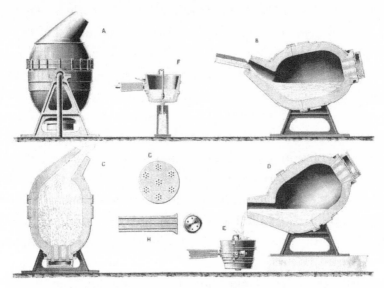

Fig. 43. The First Form of Bessemer Moveable Converter and Ladle

*A Bessemer converter used in the Bessemer process.*
*Source: https://commons.wikimedia.org*

The next step in developing steel production came during the late 1870s. Two cousins, Sidney Gilchrist Thomas and Percy Gilchrist, who were both metallurgists in Britain, came up with the idea to use dolomite or limestone as the lining of the Bessemer converter. This alone wasn't enough, so the Gilchrist cousins also added lime to the charged ore. By doing this, the chemical reaction caused additional slag to form on the melted iron, making the steel purer. An additional benefit of this new Gilchrist-Thomas process, also known as the "basic" Bessemer process (basic as in the opposite of acidic), was that phosphorus-rich slag could be recovered and sold as a phosphate fertilizer. After a while, that fertilizer became known as the Thomas meal. However, the true benefit of this addition to the original Bessemer process was the fact that for high-grade steel, it was no longer necessary to use high-grade low-phosphorus iron. From then on, it became possible to produce it from phosphorus iron, which was more common both in England and across Europe. The cousins' addition to the metallurgy technology was especially hailed in Belgium and Germany, as it made it possible for them to produce more steel. Even the US, which had high-grade iron deposits, adopted this new technology. The end result of this new step in the steel industry was that the end product was both cheaper and of higher quality. Yet it wasn't the last one.

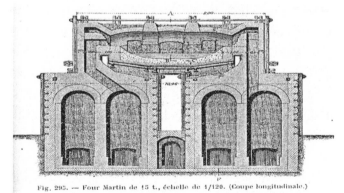

Fig. 295. — Four Martin de 15 t., échelle de 1/120. (Coupe longitudinale.)

*A Siemens-Martin or open-hearth furnace.*
*Source: https://commons.wikimedia.org*

Almost parallel with Sir Bessemer, a German inventor and industrialist who lived in England, Carl Wilhelm Siemens, began working on improving the technology of the furnace itself. His idea wasn't new, as it basically recycled waste heat. In his furnace, exhaust fumes were first directed through a brick chamber, heating the bricks to a high temperature. Then the same pathway was used to introduce hot air to the furnace, raising its temperature. While that chamber was warm enough, another was being heated by the fumes, and the two preheating chambers would alternate in use. The initial tests in 1857 were promising, and by 1861, this furnace was first put in use for glassmaking. It was a real success, as the fuel consumption was cut by about 70 percent. However, Siemens still felt it needed more work to be perfect. In the meantime, a French engineer, Pierre-Emile Martin, went on to adapt the new technology to steelmaking in 1865. Instead of battling for the patent, the two inventors agreed to share it in 1866, giving rise to the Siemens-Martin process, also known as the open-hearth process. By 1869, this new type of furnace was commercialized in three steel foundries in Britain and was slowly growing in use.

The Siemens-Martin furnace wasn't only saving fuel, but it also further raised the melting temperatures to somewhere between 2900 to 3100°F (1600 to 1700°C), which was high enough to remove almost all the impurities from the steel. Additionally, it didn't expose the steel to excessive nitrogen, which would cause steel to become more brittle, and it was easier to control. Most importantly, it allowed for a substantial amount of scrap steel to be melted and refined, introducing the idea of recycling to the steel industry. Thanks to that, and the lower fuel consumption, this type of steelmaking also lowered the cost of steel. The only drawback of the Siemens-Martin process was that it took several hours to finish. In contrast, the Bessemer process was done in about thirty minutes. Thus, the two ways of refining steel became complementary and became the staple in the steel industry up until the mid-20th century, though it's worth noting that the Siemens-Martin process became more dominant after 1910. Nonetheless, with technological contributions from across several nations, steel output in the world increased several times prior to the First World War, while the prices continued to fall. As the 19<sup>th</sup> century came to an end, steel replaced iron as the most used metal, as its use ranged from building ships, buildings, and railways to cables, machines, and boilers. Later on, even consumer goods were made out of steel.

Alongside steel, which provided the backbone for new constructions and designs in various fields, came new sources of power. The most notable and ever-important was electricity. The core concept of electricity was known for centuries around the world; however, by the early 19<sup>th</sup> century, several important scientists worked independently to give humankind a better understanding of its power. Among them were the greats such as Michael Faraday, Alessandro Volta, Hans Christian Ørsted, André-Marie Ampère, and Georg Simon Ohm. Their names remain embedded in science, as they are today used as various units, while their work helps explain the scientific basics of electricity. By 1821, Faraday even managed to create the first electric motor, giving early glimpses of what electricity was actually capable of. However, their work remained mostly unapplied until the late 19<sup>th</sup> century, which was when the concept of electricity became more widely accepted not only by scientists but also by engineers and inventors. The first step in transforming electricity from a scientific curiosity into an essential part of modern life was to find a suitable way to generate it. Once again, Faraday was a pioneer in the field. Around 1831, his generator, known as the Faraday disk, managed to produce a small DC voltage. The Faraday disk was a simple copper disk rotating between the poles of a horseshoe-shaped magnet.

Over the next couple of decades, this concept was improved by several different scientists from various nations, but it wasn't until the mid-1860s that it was improved enough for broader industrial, commercial use. It was developed simultaneously and separately by two English inventors, Sir Charles Wheatstone and Samuel Alfred Varley, as well as the German engineer and industrialist Werner von

Siemens, Carl Wilhelm's brother. Their electric generators, also known as dynamos, used rotating coils of wire around a stationary structure, which provided a magnetic field and produced electricity through induction. The rotors in these generators were first powered with water, with the first hydroelectric power station beginning operation in 1878 in England. It wasn't long before inventors realized steam could be used as well, and by early 1882, Thomas Edison opened the first coal-fueled power station in London. It used steam to rotate the mobile part of the dynamo. The marriage between the old and new energy sources came with the creation of a steam turbine by Anglo-Irish engineer Charles Parsons in 1884. Utilizing a dense set of blades, these turbines managed to extract more power than previous steam engines. Since steam turbines generate revolving motion, they are also suitable for driving the dynamo rotors. Thanks to these inventions, electricity started spreading across industrialized nations.

*Thomas Edison in the 1870s (left) and Nikola Tesla in the 1890s (right). Source: https://commons.wikimedia.org*

At the same time, numerous inventors and engineers began devising various inventions that would allow electricity to be used for everyday purposes. Among the more notable inventors was US inventor and entrepreneur Thomas Edison, whose lightbulbs revolutionized the lighting industry, taking it over from gas companies.

Apart from that, he also worked on power generation, motion picture cameras, and phonographs, setting the foundations for modern mass media. Beside him, Serbian inventor Nikola Tesla, who once worked for Edison and later became his bitter rival, devised an electric induction motor that worked on alternating current (AC), opposed to Edison's direct current (DC). This led to the so-called war of the currents in the late 1880s and early 1890s. AC power eventually won out due to its practicality, though DC is still used in various forms. Nonetheless, Tesla's induction motor meant it was possible to create multiple appliances over the next decades. Initially, this electrification was applied in various industries, producing tools and machines. Later on, in the 20th century, a wide array of consumer products was made. It is important to note that electricity was quickly adopted for use in transportation, with electric trams being used as far back as the late 1880s. Some automobile prototypes of that era also used electric motors as their power supply, but these were pushed aside by another important invention of the late 19th century: the internal combustion engine (ICE).

However, the combustion engine wasn't initially constructed for the automotive industry, for which it became synonymous. It was devised as a power supply for smaller workshops, for which steam engines were too costly and inefficient. The initial development for these engines began as far back as the late 18th century, but it wasn't until the 1870s that German inventors Nicolaus Otto and Eugen Langen managed to construct the first widely used type of the ICE. Initially, it used coal gas to cause a controlled combustion in a single cylinder, which then pushed a piston, creating kinetic energy. Later on, this and other similar engines also adopted the use of gasoline, but as electrification widened, its use died out. Nonetheless, other inventors saw its potential, most notably Karl Bentz, Gottlieb Daimler, and Wilhelm Maybach, who perfected it and miniaturized it even further so it could be used in automobiles. The first functioning and commercially available car was made by Bentz in 1886, bringing yet another revolution to transportation. The automotive industry quickly grew and spread, with France, Britain, and the US quickly following suit. The engines they used were usually powered by gasoline or, less commonly, by coal gas, while the ignition was performed by a spark plug. Then, in 1892, another German inventor, Rudolf Diesel, produced a compression-ignition, also known as the diesel engine. It took a couple of years to perfect, but this type of motor used compression to cause combustion.

*Karl Bentz's first commercially available car (right) and Henry Ford's assembly line (left). Source: https://commons.wikimedia.org*

Diesel's initial design used coal dust as fuel, but he also experimented with vegetable oils before settling for a petroleum distillate that became known as diesel fuel. However, the main advantage of a diesel engine was that it had high efficiency, making it suitable not only for cars but also for other larger transport vehicles like ships, submarines, trains, trucks, and planes. Despite the advancements in engine manufacturing, it was only in the early 1910s that cars became more widely available and affordable, thanks mostly to Henry Ford, an American industrialist and business magnate. His vision to make an automobile cheap enough for workers to own led him to pioneer the assembly line. Ford and his engineers redesigned the factory layout, machine tools, and special purpose machines so that they were all positioned in their sequence of use. Additionally, human motion was reduced by placing tools for each worker in near reach, while the products were moved via a conveyer belt between them. This was possible because, by then, electricity, electric tools, and machines were advanced enough, while interchangeable parts were already a standard in the industry. With that, true modern mass production was created. The concept itself was quickly adopted by other sectors.

The automotive industry also helped the rise of the petroleum industry. Crude oil had been used for millennia for various purposes, from making tar to its use in flammable weaponry. However, its industrial use was discovered in 1847 when Scottish chemist James Young made its first modern distillate, separating petroleum into kerosene (also known as paraffin), light oils suitable for lighting, and a heavier oil suitable for lubricating machinery. Being easy to use and relatively cheap, kerosene became the primary fuel for lighting, heating, and cooking, causing a boom in petroleum production in the late 1850s. This was helped by the fact that the modern oil refinery was devised and built by Ignacy Łukasiewicz, a Polish pharmacist working in Austro-Hungary, in 1856. At the same time, modern oil wells started popping up across the world, though it is difficult to claim which one should be the first to hold such a title. Even before Young's invention, Russian Major Alexeyev and his engineering unit hand-drilled a well in the Baku region, in modern-day Azerbaijan, in 1846. Some wells were dug or hand-drilled in Poland in 1853 and then Germany, Romania, and the Caribbean in 1857. However, the one well dug by Edwin Drake in Pennsylvania in 1859 usually gets the credit, as it was drilled with a machine powered by steam. Additionally, Drake's well caused a major explosion in the oil industry in the US.

Despite that, Imperial Russia remained the largest oil producer and exporter until the early 20th century, while the overall oil industry continued to grow. By the early 20th century, the increased demand for gasoline and diesel fuel only helped the petroleum industry to develop further, while new reservoirs were discovered around the world, like in Venezuela, Persia, Mexico, and the East Indies. The rise of the petroleum industry also helped the growth of the chemical industry; through the late 19th and early 20th centuries, various chemists created several plastic materials in part using petroleum products made through the process of polymerization. The most famous of them is PVC, which was created by accident in 1872 by a German chemist named Eugen Baumann. However, plastics remained mostly a novelty until the 1920s when they truly started being used on a grander scale. It is also worth noting that not all plastics come from oil derivates. For example, celluloid, the first plastic material created in 1856 by English inventor Alexander Parkes, and cellophane, invented by Swiss chemist Jacques Brandenberger in 1910, were both made from an organic compound called cellulose. Besides plastics, the chemical industry made other notable advances in the late 19th and early 20th centuries.

Belgian chemist Ernest Solvay devised a new process for producing soda ash in 1861, replacing the old Leblanc process. He built a tall gas absorption tower, where carbon dioxide from limestone went through salt sea brine, which produced sodium carbonate. The process was rather efficient, cheap, and capable of large-scale manufacturing. As a result, the Solvay process quickly spread across the world, considerably increasing soda ash production. At roughly the same time, the first synthetic dye, mauve, was accidentally discovered by English chemist William Henry Perkins in 1856. It was quickly adopted in the textile industry since it was a purple dye, which was hard to produce from a natural source and was therefore expensive. After its initial success, other synthetic dyes were created, changing the textile industry in the process. Another notable advance was made by the Lever brothers, who were English entrepreneurs that partnered with a chemist named William Hough Watson. Together, they started the industrial production of soap in 1885, which was based on glycerin and vegetable oils. There were numerous other inventions in this period, some of which were even tied to warfare, like the chloralkali process. Developed in the 1890s, this was a process for the industrial mass production of chlorine gas through the electrolysis of brine. However, one of the more important advances in the chemical industry came in the form of fertilizers.

The idea of adding nutritional additives to the soil wasn't new. Even during the first wave of the Industrial Revolution, some of the agriculturists in France and Germany experimented with adding gypsum to the earth. However, the first major scientific breakthrough came in 1842 when English agriculturist and entrepreneur John Bennet Lawes patented his artificial manure. After conducting experiments for years, he found that by treating phosphates with sulfuric acid, an effective fertilizer could be made. Thus, he kickstarted the artificial manure industry. The next major step was made by French chemist Jean-Baptiste Boussingault, who realized that nitrogen was the most significant ingredient in fertilizers. His experiments showed that plant growth was proportional to the volume of available absorbable nitrogen. That discovery led to the increased demand for ammonia, a compound of nitrogen and hydrogen, which was hard to synthesize in the mid-19$^{th}$ century. For the next couple of decades, there was no major breakthrough until the early 20$^{th}$ century when the fertilizer industry boomed. The first step was made in 1902 when German chemist Wilhelm Ostwald devised a method of producing nitric acid from ammonia. The nitric acid was then used for the production of fertilizer. However, the main issue remained the production of ammonia, which remained costly and difficult.

In 1903, Norwegian scientist Kristian Birkeland and his partner Sam Eyde developed the Birkeland-Eyde process. Through a chemical process known as nitrogen fixation, they produced nitric acid from atmospheric nitrogen. By achieving this, the need for ammonia was bypassed. However, this process was rather energy inefficient and was quickly replaced by a new technology developed in Germany. In 1909, a German chemist named Fritz Haber discovered a new chemical process to synthesize ammonia from atmospheric nitrogen and methane, with the help of high temperatures and metal catalysts. Later on, he received a Nobel prize for his work in this field. Yet the true potential of the Haber process was unlocked by another Nobel-awarded chemist: Carl Bosch. He continued to work on Haber's research, improving it by finding a more practical metal catalyst and designing safe high-pressure furnaces and large compressors. By 1913, he had transformed the Haber process from a tabletop experiment into a large-scale industrial manufacturing method. This is why it's sometimes called the Haber-Bosch process today. This method also caught the eye of the military industry, as ammonia could be used to produce explosives. Today, however, it remains a staple in the fertilizer industry when combined with the Ostwald process. Together, those two developments caused a major upsurge in agricultural output in the 20th century.

*Assembly of the first ammonia reactor in 1913 for the Haber-Bosch process (left) and Fritz Haber (right).*
*Source: https://commons.wikimedia.org*

Achievements in the chemical industry led to developments in other sectors as well. A great example of that is the development of the vulcanization process, a method of chemically hardening rubber with sulfur. It was independently developed by Thomas Hancock in Britain and Charles Goodyear in the US, with both patenting the same process in 1845 three weeks apart from each other. This gave rise to the modern rubber industry, as the new material proved to be quite versatile. However, the most notable contribution of vulcanization was that it made it possible to create tires. Adding a layer of rubber on wooden wheels made the chariot ride somewhat more comfortable, and in 1881, they were used on London coaches. The rubber tire fulfilled its potential when the Scottish veterinarian and inventor John Boyd Dunlop developed a pneumatic version. He technically reinvented the pneumatic tire in 1888, as there was an older, forgotten patent made by his countrymen Robert William Thomson in 1847, which never went into production. Dunlop developed the air-filled rubber tire to make his son's bicycle rides more comfortable. The new technology quickly caught on, as it coincided with the so-called bike boom. The bike itself was a new invention, designed by British engineer Harry John Lawson in 1876. After its invention, it almost immediately entered commercial production and use. By the 1890s, this new mode of transportation, which was both cheap and practical, became the latest craze.

However, the pneumatic tire, and rubber in general, saw its most symbiotic ties with the automotive industry. As automobiles were gaining in popularity as well, automobile manufacturers realized early on the advantages of fitting their cars with pneumatic tires. Additionally, rubber was also used to manufacture various car parts, for example, hoses, gaskets, and dampeners. Thus, the rubber industry, alongside the chemical industry, which aided in petrol refining, helped see the advance of the automobile in the 20$^{th}$ century. These advances were, in turn, supported by the development of tarmac and asphalt concrete. Both road surfaces had been around since ancient times, but their modern developments came in the late 19$^{th}$ and early 20$^{th}$ centuries. The idea behind them was to make a smoother driving surface by mixing sand and gravel with a binding material. In the case of tarmac, it was tar, while in asphalt concrete, it was asphalt, also known as bitumen. It's worth noting that both of these substances are linked with petroleum, with the first being its distillate and the latter a natural semi-solid state of petroleum. With smoother roads, land transportation speed rose considerably, allowing cars and trucks to achieve higher velocities.

Other modes of transport advanced as well. Railway networks grew across all nations. Thanks to cheaper steel, even the smaller and poorer countries started building their own railroads by the last years of the 19$^{th}$ century and in the early 20$^{th}$ century. On top of that, with the further advances in steam engines, trains also became faster and capable of pulling heavier weights. Water transport also advanced significantly at the same time. First, in the 1830s, the propeller was invented, and by the late 1840s, it had entered into more widespread use. With them, steamboats were able to achieve a higher speed, which was only furthered with the future advances in steam engines. Simultaneously, the vessels grew in size and carrying capacity. By the 1870s, the steam engines were perfected enough for ships to be built without sails, as they were capable of traversing vast oceans without having to stop. The next important step was substituting wood with iron and later on with steel. This led to the appearance of new types of battleships, and even the trade and cruise vessels became more durable. By the early 20$^{th}$ century, various navies started building their ships with diesel engines in them. With the digging of the Suez Canal in 1869 and the Panama Canal in 1914, the world became even more interconnected, as both waterways significantly shortened the trips to Asia and the American West Coast, respectively.

It's worth noting that by the late 19$^{th}$ century, humankind was working hard on achieving flight. There were many engineers working on conquering the skies, but it was the famous Wright brothers that made the first aerial voyage in 1903. Their Wright Flyer was the first successful controlled, heavier-than-air aircraft powered by a motor. Airplanes continued to evolve rather quickly over the next few decades. However, their full potential was only achieved after the 1930s. Thus, their influence on the Industrial Revolution was somewhat limited.

Still, with the overall advances in transportation, the world was increasingly getting smaller and more globalized. This notion of a global society was only furthered by the advancement of communication technologies. The most important invention that shaped the 19th century was the telegraph. The idea was born in the 18th century, and some initial optical telegraphs were developed, most notably in Napoleonic France. Yet the first true electromagnetic system was developed in 1833 by Carl Friedrich Gauss, a famous German mathematician and physicist, and Wilhelm Eduard Weber, another German physicist. Within a couple of years, their new system of communication was applied commercially in England. It wasn't long before telegraph lines started connecting larger cities around the world, eventually growing into a single extensive network.

*An 1830s telegraph machine with Morse code (left) and Bell's 1892 exhibition of his telephone. Source: https://commons.wikimedia.org*

By standardizing signals into the still used Morse code and by laying intercontinental lines, most notably transatlantic cable in 1866, the telegraph began connecting the entire world. Additionally, in the 1840s, Britain created a centralized post system, introducing stamps and an organized delivery system. It improved the sending of mail, adding another layer of communication to the nation, as the telegraph was only suited for short messages. The delivery speed of mail was increased when the railway started transporting official postal cargo, and trucks were also adopted by the early 20th century as a means for local transport. It wasn't long before other nations copied the British model. Nonetheless, the most notable communication advance made in the 19th century was the invention of the telephone. By the 1870s, several inventors were racing to create the functional phone, with

Alexander Graham Bell winning the race by gaining a patent for it in 1876. However, there is still some dispute over the issue, despite Bell's success both commercially and in functionality. Shortly after his achievement, in the same year, the Hungarian engineer Tivadar Puskas developed a telephone switch while working for Thomas Edison, allowing telephone networks to arise. At first, these networks were local, but by the late 19$^{th}$ and early 20$^{th}$ centuries, telephone lines crisscrossed entire countries, though the telephone remained somewhat of a higher or at least middle-class staple until after World War I.

The rise of the telegraph and telephone eased the spread of information, allowing news to travel faster than any train or automobile. However, for news to reach a wider audience, the media needed to grow with the technology. Newspapers were not only the most important but also the only media available for the entirety of the Industrial Revolution. Its initial boom, which was made by the development of the Fourdrinier papermaking machine, was only widened with new technological advances in the 1840s. German machinist Friedrich Gottlob Keller and Canadian inventor Charles Fenerty developed a device that could mechanically make pulp out of wood, making papermaking easier, faster, and cheaper. The potential of these new methods was first utilized by the newspaper industry. At roughly the same time, the steam printing press was advanced by US inventor Richard M. Hoe. In 1843, he devised a steam-powered rotary printing press. In this design, the text that would be printed was curved around a cylinder and pressed into a continuous roll of paper, making it easier to print a large amount of paper. By the 1870s, Hoe perfected the design, allowing the rotary press to print both sides of a sheet in a single process. With such advances, newspapers became increasingly cheap and widely available. By the 1900s, newspapers became the first true mass media. This was helped by the fact that literacy grew immensely over the 19$^{th}$ century.

The development of photography also helped the advance of mass media. The first successful photograph was taken in 1822 by a French inventor named Nicéphore Niépce. It was a result of the evolution of the camera obscura, with the image being etched onto a metal alloy plate coated with light-sensitive bitumen. Despite how enormously important this invention was, taking a simple photo could take hours, and the results were pale images. It's worth noting that the photographs taken by early cameras were negatives that needed to be printed on paper, and the photos themselves were black and white. Over the next couple of decades, numerous inventors and engineers worked on improving the process. By the late 1830s, British chemist John Herschel replaced the metal plates with glass that were coated with some form of light-sensitive chemicals. He coined the term "photography" and applied the terms of "positive" and "negative" to the new technology. Others improved the chemicals that were used in the process, shortening the exposure time significantly. The technology and mechanisms of the camera were also developed over the decades. By the 1870s, a photograph could be taken in less than a second. The next remarkable improvement was made by George Eastman, an American entrepreneur who founded the Kodak company. He first replaced the cumbersome glass plates with paper film in 1884, then with a plastic film made out of highly flammable nitrocellulose in 1889. Eastman also collaborated on making the cameras smaller and easier to use. After this, photography slowly became part of everyday life, and it was becoming increasingly important in the spreading of news.

The rise of photography also inspired the birth of moving pictures. The pioneers of movies were Eadweard Muybridge, an English photographer, and Émile Reynaud, a French inventor. By the late 1870s, they had created their stop-motion version of moving pictures by showing still images taken by regular cameras in quick succession. By the late 1880s, the principle was expanded, with the creation of several different movie cameras, which could take a rapid sequence of photographs on film. Probably the most famous was Edison's Kinetograph in 1891, which was designed based on the instructions by his Scottish employee William Kennedy Laurie Dickson. Not far behind was the Lumière Domitor camera, which was created by Charles Moisson in 1894 while working for the Lumière brothers, famous French cinematographers. However, despite gaining popularity as an attraction, movies remained somewhat of a novelty until after the First World War and the rise of the Hollywood movie industry.

A similar fate was shared by the radio, another invention of the late 19th century. The first step in creating a new type of communication came in 1888 when German physicist Heinrich Rudolf Hertz found conclusive evidence that electromagnetic radio waves existed. Experiments to use these new waves of communication quickly spread among inventors and scientists like Nikola Tesla, Oliver Joseph Lodge, Jagadish Chandra Bose, and Alexander Stepanovich Popov, to name a few. However, in 1896, a young Italian entrepreneur, with no engineering or scientific background, named Guglielmo Marconi patented the first wireless telegraph.

*Marconi sitting in front of his radiotelegraphy machine.*
*Source: https://commons.wikimedia.org*

Marconi didn't actually make any significant improvements on his own. He merely compiled the work of other engineers and patented it for himself. Despite that, this new form of communication quickly caught on, especially in navies, as it meant ships could communicate across the empty sea. Marconi's lack of expertise was evident when he failed to realize voice could be transmitted with radio waves, limiting his technology only for the use of Morse code. This important next step in the development of the radio was made by a Canadian inventor, Reginald Aubrey Fessenden. In the late 1900s, he made the first radio transmission of a human voice, though this is sometimes disputed, as a Brazilian priest and inventor, Roberto Landell, also made a similar transmission the same year. Nonetheless, Fessenden made the first public broadcast in 1906 of his own voice and a piece of music, which was heard by numerous ships across the Atlantic. During the early 1900s, radio technology advanced rapidly, with improvements for better antennas, amplifiers, and receivers, which were made by a number of engineers and inventors. By the eve of World War I, everything was set for radio to enter mass use. However, the war interrupted this development. Airways were reserved for the military, while the need to use headsets also lowered the practicality of radio. This changed after the Great War, and radio stations began popping up, while radio apparatus began entering households, broadcasting both the news and entertainment.

The inventions, improvements of existing technologies, and general advances mentioned so far are only some of the more notable ones, the ones that caused massive changes to the world economy. Thanks to them, the world produced more than before, was brought closer by faster travel and transport, and allowed information to be spread almost instantly. However, there were many other advances made in the same period that also changed human lives. For example, medicine developed tremendously. Louis Pasteur, a French chemist and microbiologist, discovered the principle of vaccination and, during the 1880s, made the first vaccines for rabies, chicken cholera, and anthrax. Additionally, he also invented the so-called pasteurization process, in which food is treated by mild heat to extend its shelf life by eliminating various pathogens. Vaccines prolonged human lives, while pasteurization made longer-lasting packaged food possible, allowing it to sustain extended transportation. There are other similar, though maybe less famous, examples in other disciplines as well. By 1914, the world had changed considerably, and it would be hard to mention all the inventions that had made it possible.

With the continued growth in income and production, companies expanded as well. The idea of big business became the staple in all industrialized countries by the late $19^{th}$ century. A new step was then made when firms began merging, creating conglomerates of unprecedented proportions. The most notable examples were the forming of U.S. Steel, by J. P. Morgan, who, in 1901, merged several steel companies, including one previously owned by Carnegie, into one giant corporation. It was the world's first modern billion-dollar company. A similar merger, this time of several US electric companies, was Edison's General Electric in 1892. These corporations continued to dominate their industry branches, often creating monopolies over their products or services, while their income and influence began rivaling those of some smaller states. To run them successfully, companies had to improve their bureaucracies. To achieve this, the previous style of management, which often relied solely on the prowess of its owner, was substituted by a more organized and professional operation. First of all, entire firms were broken into smaller organizational units, for example, accounting, sales, and engineering departments. Then new managerial and clerk workers, trained in running these units, were brought in. These management reforms achieved their peak with the arrival of Taylorism, named after Frederick Winslow Taylor, who advocated using scientific principles of measurement, analysis, and statistics to improve efficiency. His ideas, despite the fact they were never fully implemented, revolutionized how businesses were run from the 1890s onward.

Overall, by the First World War, the third phase of the Industrial Revolution, also called the Second Industrial Revolution, managed to reshape the world. New production methods were created, new power sources and fuels were discovered, innovative materials were developed, and new industries evolved. And unlike the first wave of industrial innovation, this time, the progress wasn't centered in one country. Industrialization was widening, and the advances made in manufacturing and technology were made by engineers, scientists, and inventors of various nationalities, making this phase of the Industrial Revolution a truly international event. More importantly, by then, the wheel of change was set in motion, and it could no longer be stopped.

# Chapter 6 – Effects of the Transformation

When we think about the Industrial Revolution, we frequently tend to focus solely on how production and the economy changed, setting inventions and advancements as our primary topic. However, no matter how defining these developments were, they were merely one part of the change brought about by industrialization. One's entire way of life was changed so much that people living in the early 1700s could relate more to their ancestors from antiquity than with their descendants from the 1900s. Thus, to fully appreciate the changes brought by the appearance of industry, we have to take a look at all the effects it had on other aspects of human existence.

The first question that typically comes to mind is how much the quality of life improved during the Industrial Revolution. It would be easy to assume it skyrocketed, as production peaked and goods became cheaper. Thus, it would be logical that the quality of life of an average human would improve drastically. However, this has become a matter of considerable debate among scholars in recent decades. One of the reasons for this disparity of opinions is different estimates for the increase of real wages, at least in the case of Great Britain. On the one hand, the more optimistic approximation states that British workers saw a roughly 50 percent increase in their real wages between 1780 and 1830. Combined with the estimated growth of the gross domestic product (GDP) of about 25 percent during the same period, this data suggests a staggering improvement of living standards in Britain. However, the pessimistic estimation halts the real wage growth at about 15 percent, which is below the GDP growth. The other aspect of this image is to position Britain in a broader European context. Even if the lowest percentage of growth is taken as being accurate, it is still higher than the rest of mainland Europe, which saw either stagnation or even a drop in real wages due to the Napoleonic Wars.

When we continue to follow the issue of wages in the 19th century, now taking into account the rest of Europe, there are some signs of an apparent salary increase. By the 1870s, there was an increase in the average income per head, which was between 50 and 200 percent when compared to the 18th century. The considerable gap between these two numbers comes from the fact that large parts of Southern and Eastern Europe weren't industrialized yet; thus, their growth was much smaller. The trend of higher income growth continued in the last phase of the Industrial Revolution until the Great War began. From these numbers, the general picture that emerges is that industrialization did, in fact, bring growth in income, even for the lower classes, yet its increase seems to have been less than stellar. In fact, it shows signs of a more gradual improvement. However, this isn't the most crucial aspect of the industrialized economy. Its greatest achievement is probably the fact that it managed to break the wage cycle. In the past, the growth in wages caused a growth in population. This, in turn, caused the lowering of salaries due to the increased workforce, which led to a population decrease. Contrary to this, with the arrival of the Industrial Revolution, both population and wages managed to continue their growth, allowing them to break out of the millennia-long deadlock.

Despite this monumental accomplishment, merely looking at the wages of this period could give a wrong idea of how hard life was for the average worker, especially in the early days of the Industrial Age. Salaries were often still so low that more than one member of a family had to work so the needs of all the family members could be sustained. And as consumerism grew, so did the need for money. In preindustrial times, at least some of the things used in the household, like, for example, clothing or basic utensils, could be homemade. This changed during the Industrial Revolution, as these items had to be bought. Thus, even though prices were falling, more items had to be purchased, adding an additional strain on the household budget. With that in mind, the wage increase may not necessarily mean a more relaxed lifestyle. The balance between the two was somewhat tipped with the arrival of mass production in the early 20$^{th}$ century. With it, prices of various items dropped considerably, while, as noted above, wages continued their steady increase, allowing for a more comfortable life, even for the average working Joe. However, the biggest strain on the household budget was food. The price of food remained relatively high, as the agricultural advances of the initial phases of the Industrial Revolution weren't enough to lower food costs. The population grew with the output, preventing a decrease in prices.

*A late 19$^{th}$-century French painting, depicting workers in a forge.*
*Source: https://commons.wikimedia.org*

While in previous times, even the lowest classes in the countryside could grow at least some food in their backyards, this became rather difficult, if not impossible, in the cities. Most of the urban working force didn't have any type of garden to plant anything besides some potted herbs. Growing their own additional food was no longer an option for them. Thus, many of the lower classes remained borderline malnourished, some even starving. These problems were somewhat lessened by the advances in railway and canal transports, as cheaper food distribution meant more affordable food. The actual breakthrough once again came in the late 19th century, with the advances in fertilizers and agricultural mechanized machinery. It was only after these developments that the majority of the population became sufficiently fed, though, of course, there were always some who remained hungry. This is corroborated by the fact that the average human height saw an increase at the time, which most scholars connect to better diets, though other environmental factors also contributed. By the early 20th century, industrialized nations no longer feared droughts and low harvests. Though they still posed a problem, they no longer threatened to crash the entire economy, which was usually the case in previous centuries. This was possible not only because of considerable surpluses that could be accumulated in good years but also because it was possible to import sufficient amounts of food from other nations or regions that hadn't been affected by the same troubles.

However, according to scholars, the best sign of decreasing malnourishment brought by the Industrial Revolution was the fact that the average life span grew from about thirty to thirty-five years in the early 18th century to around forty to forty-five years in the early 20th century. Of course, this increase wasn't solely caused by better diets. The improvements in medicine also helped, as well as infrastructural advances. For example, fresh running water was introduced in cities by the late 19th century, as water pumps powered by steam engines were used. At roughly the same time, plumbing and canalization were improved, making cities considerably cleaner. However, like with many improvements brought by the Industrial Revolution, these came in the later stages. Initially, these conditions worsened with the arrival of large-scale industry. Factories dumped their waste materials into rivers, contaminating drinking waters. Additionally, cities grew too rapidly; thus, the sewers weren't, for the most part, able to cope with the increased population. Therefore, large cities, especially ones that industrialized, were dirty, smelly, messy places. Because of that, cities became the prime place for the spreading of infectious diseases like cholera, which spread through contaminated water.

There were, of course, other conditions that affected the living situations of the lower classes during the Industrial Revolution. For one, housing posed a problem for a long time, as workers moved to the cities faster than new homes could be built. To speed the housing growth, slums and shantytowns were built. Small, simple homes, often made from cheap materials and sometimes even with dirt floors, barely covered basic living needs, if at all. To make matters worse, sometimes more than one family would live in one of these homes. That kind of crowding also contributed to the spreading of diseases, most notably tuberculosis. Compared to life in the countryside, where there was enough space, fresh air, and clean water, this was a considerable step back, yet the economic incentive was enough to continue the growth of the working class. From their perspective, if they stayed in rural areas, where there was no work, they would starve. In the cities, there was at least a chance for survival. Because of this, cities continued to grow, as industrialized nations shifted to urbanized societies. Britain and the Netherlands were the first countries where the urban population outnumbered the rural, while others, like Germany and France, achieved this later in the 19th century. The US was somewhat of an exception among the industrialized nations. Due to the agricultural economy of the South and westward expansion, its urban population outnumbered the rural only during the 1910s.

Besides the living conditions, the working class was burdened by the working conditions as well. Factories in the early Industrial Age were notoriously hazardous. Work safety was usually one of the lowest concerns for owners. Therefore, it wasn't uncommon for workers to be hurt, maimed, or even killed. Miners suffered from a similar fate. If that wasn't enough, they had to work long hours, typically anywhere between ten and twelve hours per day. To make this matter even worse, kids were often employed, both in factories and mines. As children, they were paid less. However, their smaller size made them perfect for specific jobs like going down a tight mining shaft. Thus, they were seen as a great addition to the workforce by business owners. The early years of the Industrial Revolution have left us with a substantial number of accounts of these kids getting seriously hurt. For example, a mining shaft could collapse and break some of their limbs, or their hands could get stuck in a machine that they were oiling. It wasn't uncommon for them to even be killed in these accidents. Additionally, toxic fumes, be it naturally occurring in the mines or from chemicals used in factories, would also erode their lungs or other organs, making their life an excruciating existence. For the initial phase of industrialization, kids suffered as much as their parents, whose lives were similarly endangered.

*Illustration showing an 18th-century child miner (left) and kids working in an early 20th-textile factory (right).*
*Source: https://commons.wikimedia.org*

However, by the 1830s, this started to change a bit, at least in Britain. Small kids were slowly being banned from working, while teenagers had their hours limited. Additionally, with the development of new production technologies, their roles in the textile industry were somewhat cut out, as machines were becoming increasingly automated. Thanks to these factors, child labor started to decrease. Still, it existed throughout the 19th century, although new laws began to regulate it even tighter. Thanks to that, as well as other improvements in medicine, housing, and nutrition, the child mortality rate started to drop significantly over the course of the century, adding yet another reason why the life expectancy and population numbers were rising. Despite that, working conditions for adults remained hazardous, though even their position got better, but not without some friction. While owners wanted cheap laborers who would work from dusk till dawn, without investing in their safety, workers wanted the opposite. The initial backlash for the introduction of machines, which was initially seen as taking human jobs, was slowly transformed into protests for better working conditions. These were the seeds of trade unions and the class struggle that was brought about by industrialization.

Before the Industrial Revolution, society was generally divided into three classes: the aristocracy, the clergy, and the peasants. However, ever since the Middle Ages, this concept was slowly unraveling. The power of the aristocracy lay in its wealth that came from large properties; however, through the centuries, other ways to earn substantial amounts of money emerged. The most notable was perhaps trading, yet merchants never managed to fully dislodge the nobles from their top social position. However, with the arrival of industrial manufacturing, entrepreneurs and industrialists quickly started earning a lot. As a new motor of the economy, their power and importance quickly grew, and they began overthrowing the aristocrats on the social ladder. Initial investors and industrialists indeed came from noble families, as they were the only ones who had enough capital to finance new industrial endeavors, but most of the aristocrats were uninterested in such gambles. As the first phase of the Industrial Revolution continued, new entrepreneurs emerged without a noble background. By the early 19th century, successful industrialists became more powerful than landowning aristocrats. The two classes mingled throughout the century, but the nobles were rapidly losing their positions. Businessmen and factory owners started to rule the world as the new high class of society.

The clergy, which was once below the aristocrats, was also failing to remain an essential part of society. The priests were once the pinnacle of educated strata, backed by the Church, a powerful organization that usually worked closely with the state. However, as education began to expand during the Industrial Revolution, a new educated class emerged. It consisted of the managers and clerks, doctors and lawyers, and teachers and engineers. They became known as the middle class. The clergy was unable to sustain their importance, as it couldn't fulfill the new roles needed in society. Additionally, its conservativism made it rather hard for them to accept the new evolving society, and religion was also slowly being replaced by science in the search for the answers to the important life questions. Finally, the Industrial Revolution also dislodged the position of the peasants. Prior to the Industrial Revolution, farmers were the core of production. And not only did they engage in agriculture, but they also produced various other products, like clothes or carpentry. Of course, these items weren't always meant for sale, and part of the peasants still depended on the aristocrats, becoming land tenants. This changed with the arrival of industry, as the new means of production meant that agriculture no longer held the top position in the economy, while the masses began emigrating from the countryside to the cities in search of a better life.

Workers in various industry branches took over as the main producing class of this changing society. The Industrial Revolution was carried through the hard work of the laborers in mines and factories. However, they were constantly degraded and looked down upon by their employers. Although by the early 20th century, an average worker lived better than in the mid-18th century, at least in the grand scale of things, their benefits were marginal compared to the businessmen. While the industrialists had villas and automobiles, the workers still lived in tiny homes, ate sparsely, and worked long hours for little pay. In fact, it seems that during the Industrial Revolution, the wealth disparity between the classes grew, regardless of the overall economic growth. To make matters worse for the workers, they had regular contact with their higher-class supervisors, unlike in the previous times when oppressed peasants rarely saw their feudal oppressors. The bubbling dissatisfaction with watching others benefiting from the yield of their hard work continued to grow, and the laborers began revolting, demanding better pay, shorter hours, and better working conditions. However, the industrialists usually had the backing of the state, as most countries supported big business as their national economic strategy. Thus, worker strikes were often put down violently, sometimes with lethal force. In turn, the protesters themselves sometimes turned toward more radical means and forceful protests.

*An 1880s painting of a factory workers' strike.*
*Source: https://commons.wikimedia.org*

By the 1840s, the now-notorious German philosopher Karl Marx began forming his new ideology based on the class struggle. From his point of view, the clash between the exploited workers and the exploiting owners was inevitable, as the laborers had the right to own the means of production to form a more equal and just society. From these ideas arose new political theories, like socialism and communism. Though in various degrees, these related ideologies both had the goal of the state or society taking control of all of the production, both industry and agriculture, and spreading the gains evenly. The utopian ideal was a society without classes, money, and, ultimately, a state where all men and women lived in equality. As this was anti-capitalist, anti-monarchist, and anti-religious, supporters of these political parties were dealt with harshly by most authorities in the industrialized countries. Ironically, this ideology, which was devised for highly industrialized nations, came to power for the first time in the still relatively undeveloped and agrarian Russia, which became the Soviet Union in 1917. This set the stage for the clash between socialist and capitalist nations over the course of the $20^{th}$ century. Nonetheless, even in capitalist countries, the class struggle brought some rewards for the workers.

Over the course of the $19^{th}$ century, through strikes and protests, workers managed to shorten their workday to eight hours, get safer working conditions, and, in some cases, gain access to some benefits like basic healthcare and pensions. Additionally, even though many countries initially banned them, workers fought to establish their right to unionize. This meant that laborers would be organized in large groups, making it harder for business owners to exploit them. However, these workers' unions never managed to fully integrate into a countrywide association. There were just too many difficulties and differences between the various laborers to achieve this, leaving mostly local unions covering maybe a single city or even a single factory. It is also worth noting that besides rebelling against their exploitative owners, they also sometimes clashed with each other. Sometimes this happened between two competing factories, and sometimes it was against the immigrants who were seen as taking jobs from the locals. The latter was the most common in the US. It was also not uncommon for the explosion of riots to occur when the price of bread rose. Forced by sheer misery, they would direct their anger on the bakers. However, with the improvements in living conditions in the early $20^{th}$ century, these violent revolts toned down, though peaceful protests and strikes remained a valid form of fighting for one's rights.

These forms of nonviolent protest were also used by another disenfranchised portion of the population to fight for their rights.

Over the 19th century, in the Western nations, women began their search for equality with men. They asked for the right to vote, equal job opportunities and salaries, and easier access to education, ownership, and much else. An illustration of just how bad a woman's position was in society can be seen in the 1869 essay, *The Subjection of Women*, by John Stuart Mill, an English philosopher and civil servant. In it, he compares women to slaves, as she is almost a bondservant to her husband or men of the house. Though some men, like Mill, supported women's rights, most dismissed them, asking their wives to stay home. This prompted women to campaign for their equality. They organized rallies, protests, and social gatherings, forming various organizations and associations to further their cause. The most notable and well known were the suffragette associations that advocated for the political right to vote. Though these movements were the strongest in Great Britain and the US, the first nation to give women the right to vote was New Zealand in 1893, which acted as a self-governing British colony. From then on, women's rights started spreading, first in Australia, then in Europe. By 1918, several European nations, including Britain, Russia, and Germany, had given women the right to vote. This was achieved in the US in 1920.

Despite that, it should be noted that the equality of women in society was not achieved by gaining suffrage. The women's rights movement continued its fight for equality throughout the 20th century and even today. However, the timing of this historical development poses the question of how the Industrial Revolution affected the position of women in general. Like with the matter of classes, scholars are divided on this issue. On the one hand, the negativist interpretation states that industrialization actually pushed women away from equality. Before the Industrial Revolution, women played important roles in production, be it on farms or in textile manufacturing, but the birth of industry left them at home, as men more often went out to work. This happened because new machines and jobs usually required more strength, making it generally impractical to hire a woman to do the job. Thus, a number of women were reduced to the role of an unpaid house servant, stuck with household obligations. Of course, many lower-class women had to take jobs, but since they were seen as less capable and skilled, they were paid considerably less. This prompted the creation of the wage gap, which still exists today. The higher-class ladies didn't have to work, yet they were still expected to run the household and servants and act as obedient wives to the male breadwinners.

*Early 19th-century painting depicting a woman tied up to a wall, sewing (left) and early 20th-century women protesting for their suffrage rights.*
*Source: https://commons.wikimedia.org*

In this interpretation, the betterment of women's positions came through the general enlightenment of society, which was inspired by the general advancement of human rights, and the Industrial Revolution only worsened the circumstances. On the other hand, a more positivist interpretation actually claims the Industrial Revolution helped the women's rights movement. In this view, preindustrial production was usually home-based, and while women were involved, they didn't have direct control of the income, as that belonged to the men. However, with the arrival of industry, women started having jobs outside their homes, and they themselves were getting paid. Since families depended on this additional income, and since women directly contributed, their status began to improve. Finally, by the late stages of the Industrial Revolution, women were more widely employed and often had more direct control of their lives. Thus, by allowing women to gain at least some financial independence, the Industrial Revolution allowed them to tackle the matter of their own rights head-on. Yet despite what interpretation one leans to, it is important to note that the women's rights movement was mainly carried by middle-class or high-class ladies since they had the privilege of having enough time and education to take on the struggle. Lower-class women were usually too concerned with making ends meet to contribute significantly to the cause.

*A scarred Mississippi slave from the 1860s (left) and an 18th-century abolitionist medallion (right). Source: https://commons.wikimedia.org*

Another important issue to consider is the Industrial Revolution's impact on slavery. One's logic might be that, with the rise of machine production and mechanized agriculture, the need for slavery would die down. New technology usually did require a skilled laborer, which was something most slaves weren't. There is some truth in this, but it was not so much because of the lesser need for human labor but because it proved to be more profitable to deal with industry than with slaves. However, it seems that early industrialization, with its focus on the cotton textile industry, actually had the opposite effect. While the machines for textile manufacturing and cotton processing evolved, they increased the demand for raw cotton. However, there was no technology for harvesting raw cotton, which was a labor-intensive process. Thus, this prompted numerous colonial landowners across the Americas to invest in more slaves to meet the high demand. As slavery saw somewhat of an increase in the late $18^{th}$ and early $19^{th}$ centuries, in Europe and the northern industrialized states of the US, the practice of slavery was banned and/or abolished. At certain times, some nations, such as France during the French Revolution, tended to outlaw slavery in the homeland while allowing it in their colonies, where most, if not all, slaves were exploited. In practice, the need for cheap labor outweighed morals.

Despite that, in about the 1820s, antislavery as an idea began to see rapid growth, and political battles started to brew in numerous nations. The most notable are, of course, Britain and the US. In Britain, the empire-wide abolition of slavery came in 1833. Yet, due to India's particular legal position in the empire, slavery remained legal in parts of India until the 1860s. In the US, slavery saw a nationwide ban only after the end of the Civil War in 1865. Around this time, most nations, including the less industrial countries of South America and Eastern Europe, also banned slavery, indicating that industrial development had little to do with such a decision. It seems that the abolition of slavery was more based on the development of the enlightenment ideas of justice and equality than with advances in technology. Still, the Industrial Revolution created an atmosphere where abolition was possible. As mentioned before, it led to broader and more available education while also showing that profit without slave labor was not only possible but also higher. In the end, the Industrial Revolution had a mixed influence on this matter. Despite that, it should be noted that the 19th century, regardless of abolitionism and enlightened ideals, was filled with racism and the exploitation of local colored populations across the continents, which continued well into the 20th century, leaving traces of it in modern society as well.

*Depiction of a typical Industrial Revolution scenery with smoke rising from factory chimneys. Source: https://commons.wikimedia.org*

Another negative trend started by the Industrial Revolution that is still present is pollution and its effects on the environment. Before the development of industry, humans barely affected the ecology. They did chop down forests and deposed of their trash in the rivers and oceans, but most of their waste was degradable and ultimately unharming to the environment. However, with the arrival of coal-burning steam engines, air pollution became a rising issue. In a matter of decades, cities became covered in smog and smoke. Nonetheless, not many argued about it initially, as it was seen as a sign of progress. Later on, with the increased use of various chemicals in the textile industry, rivers became the primary place for toxic waste disposal. This only worsened as new industries were created, most notably the chemical and gas industries, which produced increasingly toxic byproducts. By the mid-19th century, governments started noticing the effects of pollution, prompting early regulations. However, these were mostly local and inefficient. Since industry was essential for economic expansion, no government wanted to impede its development and growth too much. This led to the forming of a number of associations and organizations fighting for environmental preservation in the late 19th century. The ecological impact of the Industrial Revolution also turned a portion of the population against industrialization. Nevertheless, industry continued to damage the environment, while governments did only the bare minimum to stop them.

The arrival of the Industrial Age brought another important change to the modern way of life that we usually take for granted. With the increased manufacturing output, growing urbanization, rising population, and overall growth of the economy, a new economic branch emerged. Aptly named the service sector, this branch was tasked not with production but with providing services to those who were able to pay. These jobs had existed for millennia, most notably in the forms of taverns and even lawyers, but with the arrival of the Industrial Age, the need for such businesses grew. With the growing nightlife, more and more inns and restaurants were opened, while easier travel increased the demand for hotels. New jobs were also created, like telephone operators. Growing businesses also needed clerks, secretaries, and low-level managers, while even governmental bureaucracies required such professionals. These so-called white-collar jobs essentially became the backbone of the middle class. Not only were the salaries usually better, at least when compared to equally skilled laborers, but they also required little to no physical work. This was especially important in regard to women, as it meant they were more than equally capable of doing the jobs as men. It is likely no coincidence that the service sector's growth coincided with the emergence of the women's rights movement. However, the most crucial aspect of this change is that it brought a much higher diversity to the economy, helping it grow and expand into new areas and allowing for more capital to be created.

In the end, the Industrial Revolution changed almost every aspect of human life. On the one hand, the work-life of the majority became tightly run and well organized, much stricter than it had been in the preindustrial age. Factory workers had to obey more rules and procedures, and while they were working, their lives were essentially run by others. Alongside the increasingly rigid work-life, the rising income also brought new leisure opportunities, which became vital for the massive urban workforce. After a long day on the job, laborers wanted to let off some steam. They sought fun and recreation in pubs and popular music theaters, better known as vaudevilles, and tourism, as we know it today, was created. Movies and recorded music only furthered this change. Excess capital formed by the Industrial Revolution also helped in the creation of modern and professional sports, establishing yet another possibility for the working class to escape the everyday drudgery of life. Even art became more widely available, as mass production allowed for cheap books, paintings, vases, and sculptures. Despite the argument that art became watered down or kitsch, the fact remains that it wasn't available only to the wealthiest class anymore. It is also worth noting that the Industrial Age produced some of the most notable artists in history, like Vincent Van Gogh and Leo Tolstoy, just to mention a few. Art itself was changed when some artists tried to encapsulate the grit of industrial times. In contrast, others found art as an escape to nature, which was becoming ever more distant from human existence.

All of these changes were not only brought on by the newly gained excess capital but also by the technological advances of the Industrial Revolution itself. Steamships and trains allowed people to travel, concrete and steel were needed to build stadiums, artificial paint made painting cheaper and easier, and the printing press could make thousands of books a day. If that wasn't enough, even the very way of life was changed by the Industrial Revolution. Homes were built from bricks and concrete, as well as steel and glass. Their design, at least for the cheaper housing, became simpler and was usually reproducible on a large scale. Almost all of the items inside the homes were now made in a factory by someone else, bought with wages earned by hard work. Consumerism was thriving, helped by the arrival of mass production and department stores. With it came new ways of selling things, as advertisements covered more and more of the city landscape. Lives started around selling, buying, and owning things. Yet thanks to a much wider variety of available consumer goods, many found it easier to express their own identities. They could choose what clothes to wear, what newspapers to read, and what music to listen to. Unfortunately, these choices were often dictated by current fads, leaving many leading similar lives.

Finally, the Industrial Revolution sped up human lives. On the one hand, as one's value was increasingly seen only through currency, time became money. It was seen as inadequate to waste time too much, and so, everyone started hurrying. This was only facilitated by increasingly fast transportation and communication. Though leisure activities grew, there was less and less time for it. That is one of the reasons why it became so important to find a good way to fill it. It was almost as if everyone was chasing something. The hectic nature of urban life only added to such feelings, as streets became crowded, and life became increasingly complicated. Like machinery, everything seemed to have more cogs and moving parts. The new way of life brought new kinds of pressure, feelings of loneliness, and a sense of disconnection from fellow humans. Yet, at the same time, it made everything much more exciting and snappier. Everything was instant, and nothing could wait. Flavors became bolder, colors much brighter. In the end, like for most things in life, the experience of the Industrial Revolution depended on one's point of perspective and personal experience.

# Epilogue

It isn't uncommon for books about the Industrial Revolution to end their stories on the eve of the First World War. Ending on a high note, where the industry is booming and everything is fine, is always a popular choice. However, it is crucial to recognize that history isn't as clean and joyful as we sometimes try to represent it. The increasing power and wealth wielded by the increasingly competitive industrial states are at least partially responsible for the eruption of the Great War. Even if the connection is questionable, the high death toll and massacres that ensued over the four years of bloody combat are undeniably the product of the Industrial Age. New types of weapons, which were deadlier than ever before, were produced in unprecedented quantities. This was all thanks to the numerous technological advances made during the Industrial Revolution. Industrialization also partly contributed to the creation of a new type of warfare, known today as total war. Whereas in prior times, it was enough to knock out enemy troops to win, with the modern industrial economy and increased population, an entire army could be quickly replaced by a new unit. Thus, it wasn't enough to kill the enemy but also to devastate its economy, civilian population, and entire home front to be able to achieve a clear, decisive victory. Unfortunately for humanity, this wasn't achieved in 1918, and a new world war erupted in 1939, which proved to be even bloodier. Again, even more advanced industries made this possible.

The fact that industry continued to develop after 1914 also poses a question if the Industrial Revolution ever truly ended. It is worth noting that a number of scholars tend to say no and actually claim that the revolution is continuing to this day. In their eyes, with the new significant breakthrough in technologies achieved in the 1950s and 1960s, the world entered a Third Industrial Revolution. New types of plastics were created, steel production was once again improved, consumer goods became cheaper, and a new cornerstone in production and income was achieved. By the late 20$^{th}$ century, with the arrival of computers and the digital age, another technological leap was made. Computers made everything run smoother, while robotics began replacing the increasingly inefficient human labor even more than before. The internet made communication both instant and worldwide. Another significant industrial advance was achieved in what can be seen as the Fourth Industrial Revolution. Throughout the 20$^{th}$ and early 21$^{st}$ centuries, substantial improvements and developments were made in production materials, like carbon fibers, or in energy, with nuclear and solar plants. All this does confirm the idea that the Industrial Revolution never truly ended. However, it is also true that these changes, no matter how vital, were not as revolutionary as the arrival of industrialization. The Industrial Revolution, in a way, turned into an evolution since technology continued to advance.

That being said, this point of view is somewhat Western-centric, as it applies only to the nations that were industrialized by the early 20$^{th}$ century. While those countries no longer experience these changes as revolutionary, a number of Asian, African, East European, and South American nations didn't start their industrialization movement until after 1918. From their viewpoint, the Industrial Revolution didn't end until they had transformed their economies as well. It is enough to think about China, a top economic rival of the US in the modern day, which only started to industrialize in the 1950s, achieving significant breakthroughs only in the 1990s. The fact is that there are still a great number of countries waiting for their industrial rebirth, something that most nations gravitate to since, so far, it is a prerequisite for economic prosperity. Understanding that leads to the idea that the Industrial Revolution never stopped, as it is still spreading across the globe. Thus, with the continuing technological advances and spreading of industry, the Industrial Revolution hasn't truly found its end, even though its nature has changed significantly over the two and a half centuries since its beginning. This is only corroborated by the fact that our lives today continue to be impacted and altered by the transformations in manufacturing and the economy.

# Conclusion

The Industrial Revolution covered a long period and a lot of countries. It was a single centralized event, like most through history, and its effect on entire humankind is hard to measure. Production skyrocketed, the population grew, machines started replacing humans, science and education evolved, society was transformed, and everyday life was altered. Almost nothing remained the same. Like many historical events of such complexity, the Industrial Revolution is hard to evaluate. It had positive as well as negative effects on humankind, both objectively and from particular perspectives and viewpoints. Yet this shouldn't come as a surprise, as life is rarely clear-cut and simple. Understanding that helps us understand our modern time, especially since its complexity was built upon the foundations laid by the Industrial Revolution itself. Understanding the forces that caused the rise of industry, and later helped evolve it, also helps us understand our own present. In the end, it is what history is all about, trying to fathom all the complexities of the past and trying to extrapolate it on our times. If we are able to see both the positive and negative sides of our history, we can better assess our own age in an objective manner, no matter how grim or bright the aspects of our present days may seem at certain times.

Another lesson that can be learned from the Industrial Revolution is that change is neither good nor bad but a regular part of our existence. We shouldn't fear it, but we also should not let ourselves do things to create change without any thought or control. And when the transformation has begun, there is rarely anything we can do to stop it. History tends to tell us that this is true, no matter if the change is small or big, quick or slow, or instantaneous or long-lasting. The revolution that came with industrialization was, by all means, huge, fast, and long, adding to its complexity. The change was so profound that it affected every part of our lives. It could be compared to the biological example of the first animal walking on land many million years ago. In essence, it was the Industrial Revolution that almost singlehandedly brought our society into modernity. As such, it is tough to attempt to encapsulate every aspect of such an event in a satisfactory manner. Because of that, this book is merely an introduction to the story of the Industrial Revolution, something that has hopefully sparked your interest in reading more about this instrumental historical event.

# Bibliography

Brinley Thomas, *The Industrial Revolution and the Atlantic Economy: Selected Essays*, London, Routledge, 1993.

C. Freeman and Francico Louçã, *As time goes by: From the Industrial Revolutions to the Information Revolution*, Oxford, Oxford University Press, 2001.

Charles R. Morris, *The First American Industrial Revolution: The Dawn of Innovation*, New York, PublicAffairs, 2012.

Craig Calhoun, *The Question of Class Struggle: Social Foundations of Popular Radicalism during the Industrial Revolution*, Chicago, University of Chicago Press, 1982.

Douglas Fisher, *The Industrial Revolution: A Macroeconomic Interpretation*, London, The Macmillan Press LTD, 1992.

E.A. Wrigley, *Energy and the English Industrial Revolution*, Cambridge, Cambridge University Press, 2010.

Emma Griffin, *Liberty's Dawn: A People's History of the Industrial Revolution*, New Haven, Yale University Press, 2013.

Eric J. Hobsbawm, *Industry and Empire: From 1750 to the Present Day*, London, Penguin Books, 1999.

Graeme Donald Snooks, *Was the Industrial Revolution Necessary?*, London, Routledge, 1994.

Hal Marcovitz, *The Industrial Revolution*, San Diego, ReferencePoint Press, Inc., 2014.

J. Horn, L. N. Rosenband and M. R. Smith, *Reconceptualizing the Industrial Revolution*, Cambridge, The MIT Press, 2010.

James R. Farr, *World Eras vol. 9: Industrial Revolution in Europe, 1750-1914*, Detroit, Thomas Gale, 2003.

James Wolfe, *The Industrial Revolution: Steam and Steel*, New York, Britannica Educational Publishing, 2016.

Jane Humphries, *Childhood and Child Labour in the British Industrial Revolution*, Cambridge, Cambridge University Press, 2010.

Joel Mokyr, *The British Industrial Revolution: An Economic Perspective*, Boulder, Westview Press, 1999.

Joyce Burnette, *Gender, Work and Wages in Industrial Revolution Britain*, Cambridge, Cambridge University Press, 2008.

K. Hillstrom and L. C. Hillstrom, *The Industrial Revolution in America: Iron and Steel, Railroads, Steam Shipping*, Santa Barbara, ABC-CLIO, 2005.

Kenneth E. Hendrickson III, *The Encyclopedia of the Industrial Revolution in World History*, London, Rowman & Littlefield, 2015.

Laura L. Frader, *The Industrial Revolution: A History in Documents*, Oxford, Oxford University Press, 2006.

Lawrence Barham, *From Hand to Handle: The First Industrial Revolution*, Oxford, Oxford University Press, 2013.

Lee T. Wyatt III., *The Industrial Revolution*, London, Greenwood Press, 2009.

Michael Andrew Žmolek, *Rethinking the Industrial Revolution: Five Centuries of Transition from Agrarian to Industrial Capitalism in England*, Boston, Brill, 2013.

Pat Hudson, *The Industrial Revolution*, London, Hodder Arnold, 2005.

Peter N. Stearn, *The Industrial Revolution in World History*, Boulder, Westview Press, 2013.

Phyllis Deane, *The First Industrial Revolution*, Cambridge, Cambridge University Press, 1979.

R. M. Hartwell, *The Causes of the Industrial Revolution in England*, New York, Routledge, 2017.

Richard Grassby, *The Idea of Capitalism before the Industrial Revolution*, London, Rowman & Littlefield, 1999.

Robert C. Allen, *The British Industrial Revolution in Global Perspective*, Cambridge, Cambridge University Press, 2009.

Robert C. Allen, *The Industrial Revolution: A Very Short Introduction*, Oxford, Oxford University Press, 2017.

Robert J. Morris, *Class and Class Consciousness in the Industrial Revolution, 1780- 1850*, London, The Macmillan Press LTD, 1979.

Roger Osborne, *Iron, Steam & Money: The Making of the Industrial Revolution*, London, The Bodley Head, 2013.

S. Broadberry and K. H. O'Rourke, *The Cambridge Economic History of Modern Europe Volume 1 and Volume 2*, Cambridge, Cambridge University Press, 2010.

Stanley Chapman, *Merchant Enterprise in Britain: From the Industrial Revolution to World War I*, Cambridge, Cambridge University Press, 1992.

Sylvia Jenkins Cook, *Working Women, Literary Ladies: The Industrial Revolution and Female Aspiration*, Oxford, Oxford University Press, 2008.

Vaclav Smil, *Creating the Twentieth Century: Technical Innovations of 1867–1914 and Their Lasting Impact*, Oxford, Oxford University Press, 2005.

William J. Ashworth, *The Industrial Revolution: The State, Knowledge and Global Trade*, London, Bloomsbury Academic, 2017.

Here's another book by Captivating History
that you might be interested in

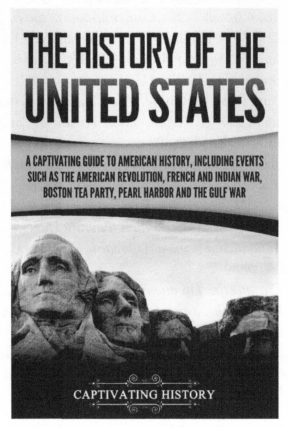

Made in the USA
Monee, IL
23 April 2021